ULTIMATUS

a gaming corporation

A. A. Dober

For Lorraine:
The love of my life.

And to my boy and girl for their ideas,
avatar names, and gaming advice.

Many thanks

Norma Peabody
Brendan Myers
Ronald Nadzam
Alexandra Zelman
Ryan McBride
Mike Rossbacher

And thanks to my editor,
HappyMarli

ULTIMATUS

Key to Main Characters		
PLAYERS		
Name	**Avatar**	**Country**
Noah Jones	Noah88	USA
Gina Gazzoni	BlingBlingBaby	Italy
Simon Prince	Slowpry (shared)	USA
Mark Sloan	Slowpry (shared)	USA
Fellini	Fellini	
Ricardo Rodriguez	SodaPop	Mexico
Stellan Boström	Firemist1	Sweden
Ming Lin	HappySpirit	China
NON-PLAYERS		
Name	**Occupation**	**Country**
Director Robert Stewart	CIA Director	USA
Eric Bergstrom	Chief Detective Inspector Stockholm Police	Sweden
Ingeborg Larsson	Detective Inspector Stockholm Police	Sweden
William Ramel	IT Expert Stockholm Police	Sweden
Robert Lang	MI-6 operative	England
Mrs. Ratner	Secretary to Director Stewart at the CIA	USA
Pedro Diaz	CIA operative in the Azores Islands; also in Azores Police	Portugal

1

Inside the computer game, there was an eerie
resemblance to life in a modern city. In this virtual reality,
the environment was futuristic, somewhat reminiscent of
the visual reality of Brazil. The arenas were cities filled
with modern buildings, yet overrun by vegetation and the
detritus of humanity. The government, if any could be said
to exist, was in a state of disarray—its absence all too
evident. The surrealist painter Giorgio de Chirico, who
famously captured the absence of God, could have been
the designer behind the stark, barren spaces that Noah
explored. His avatar was called Noah88, and he was
running across the pavement near an old aqueduct,
entering every arch, and slamming his virtual body on the
concrete piers to protect himself from the potential
onslaught of enemy gunfire.

Noah88 held a gun and raced with clear purpose.
Ahead of him, past the aqueduct, lay a field and a tall,
blocky structure behind a fence. Two men were guarding a
gate that ran along the fence. Noah88 opened fire at the
two uniformed officers guarding what had just become
visible on the screen: a sprawling modern villa surrounded

by a cheap chain-link fence. The guards died quickly, bullet-riddled, before they even had a chance to shoot back. The kill was replayed in slow motion on a small PiP (picture-in-picture) on Noah Jones's flat screen.

Now that was cool.

Noah88 grabbed the chain-link fence and pushed against it. The lock on the chain did not budge, so he tried to jump the fence instead. The height of his jump capability was limited, meaning that he can't clear the fence that way. He thought that there might be a clue inside the house that he needed. Looking at the landscape in his immediate vicinity, he spotted a semi-hidden police car. In the game, the image on the screen seamlessly shifted between POV (point of view), an angle behind Noah's avatar, and a BEV (bird's-eye view). In all three camera views, Noah88 tried the jump, hoping for a happy glitch, but he couldn't make it. He moved back to the bodies of the fallen officers and searched for a key to the gate lock. The only keys were attached to a chain on the belt loop of one cop; Noah88 picked them up, but none of them work. He zoomed in for a closer view and noticed that they are car keys.

I can use the cop car to ram the gate, although I might make too much noise. Maybe I can just move it enough to . . . .

He quickly entered the police car and started it. The engine roared to life, noisy and powerful—a sound Noah was trying to avoid. He slowly moved the car forward so the hood was just touching the fence and then turned the engine off. Without closing the door, he silently got out of the car, leaped onto the hood, and then over the fence. As Noah88 ran to the front door of the villa, the zinging noise of bullets was hot on his heels. He ducked right, but instead of turning around to shoot back, he jumped and hit the front door squarely. The door opened on impact, and he rolled into the safety of the house. The whole screen lit up, and Noah smiled happily.

Another level cleared.

The ceremony began and a small movie-like sequence appeared on the screen. Passing that level meant that Noah was eligible for a new title and a few more elite abilities. He has become a Spielberg-level player. Noah turned the computer off, knowing that he could rest for a while. His body was covered in sweat, and he reached for the towel he always kept next to him while playing.

Noah flipped on the light switch as his computer went into sleep mode. His eyes adjusted, and the old stucco walls of his Lower East Side NYC apartment, which he rented at an unreasonably high $1,500 a month, came into focus. He was wearing his Ultisuit, a strange system of cables that stretched from his ankles and wrists to a small pack on his back. His shirtless body was chiseled like a Navy Seal's. He glanced at a pair of wall clocks: one with NY written above it and the other with GMT etched over it in black Helvetica lettering.

Shit. It's almost six. Work in fifteen minutes.

Noah needed to move fast. He rushed through every routine movement, dressed, squirted on some cologne, and turned the three locks of his trashy apartment door as fast as possible. He kept his ten-speed bike in the cramped hallway and practically tore the lock off the stair rail in his rush. Noah hung his messenger bag on his hip and descended the stairs with the bicycle on his shoulder. Being a bike messenger in NYC was just as dangerous as the game he played but was decidedly less important. The income stream was what made all the difference. Noah was trying to prove to his family back in San Diego that he could survive in NYC all by himself;

not only that, he wanted to show that he was able to really become someone. In the game, he was already making his mark, so redemption and actual proof might be close. Noah was looking forward to achieving the ultimate gamer goal: paid gaming.

The invitation to the tournament should be coming soon. If I can start getting paid to play before I'm twenty, they'll finally see what I'm capable of . . . .

***

Ondrej and Lucie Lorenc had been married for twenty-seven years, but their lives had been primarily bound by their son, Marek. They were sitting in the decrepit police department of 357 Sumna Road in Liberec, Czech Republic, which was a small, quaint city in the middle of nowhere, both literally and figuratively. Dressed as if they had been wearing their clothes for weeks, rubbing red, swollen, and exhausted eyes with bags beneath them, they waited in silence. The mid-level detective approached—the two figures were anguished and distraught. Detective Radko Drabic was aware of the situation, but his gut told him that something was truly wrong this time; the pair looked awful.

"Our son has been gone for over a year now. What's the matter with your service, Radko? This is not normal. There has to be some information somewhere," Ondrej said, clearly frustrated.

"Interpol has his passport number on watch, but nothing has been reported. We know that he took that flight to Marseille, but that's it. I don't know what to tell you. He has simply . . . vanished. Maybe you had some sort of fight with him?" Radko answered and then asked gently, trying to deflect a bit of responsibility.

"Ondrej always fought with Marek . . . always . . . . But he called daily. Something has happened. My son would never suddenly stop calling me! Never!" Lucie interrupted.

"I'm sorry, Lucie, I didn't mean to imply that. There is simply nothing I can do. You need a private investigator to go to France and ask some questions . . . I don't know. Perhaps show his picture around the streets," Radko explained.

"With what money?" Ondrej raised his hands helplessly.

"I am finished with this. I will go myself," Lucie stated furiously, tears in her eyes.

Lucie stormed out of the station, leaving Ondrej with his face buried in his hands, sobbing in front of Detective Radko's desk. She knew that traveling to France and searching for their son was irrational and impossible, but she was tired of looking on the Internet and finding nothing—nothing but thin air.

2

Gina Gazzoni was a tall Italian woman, only twenty-three years of age, with dazzling blue eyes and strawberry-blonde hair. On this particularly sunny summer day, she wore a tight black skirt, a tight white T-shirt, and expensive Ferragamo flats. Beautiful and strikingly athletic, she moved with a strong, confident pace, an attitude that screamed, *"Do not speak to me. Do not stand in my way."* Her shoes tapped the cobblestone streets of Florence in a steady, fast pace.

Italy was overflowing with men looking for young women, which encouraged Italian females like Gina to adopt that forceful, no-nonsense body language. She entered a stunning antique building, pushing past the large wooden door after typing in a five-digit code. Inside, an old elevator was nestled beside the staircase that led to her apartment on the top floor. From her apartment, there was a view of Via Sorrento; the famous Ponte Vecchio, atop the Arno River, posed quietly in the background.

Gina had achieved Visconti-level in the game and had been to the tournament three times. Skill and instinct combined in a way that she could have never imagined to take her to the heights she had reached. A professional player and a paid gamer, she was now hurrying home to meet her mother, who would surely be waiting for her already.

As a youngster, she had adored playing video games with her brothers and loved to keep electronic pets. Early on, her studies were dedicated to computer science and web design; a love of Pascal and DOS computer languages had enabled her to graduate early and achieve a college degree at only nineteen. Now, four years later, her proudest accomplishment was that she no longer needed to work for anyone but herself. She had achieved financial independence doing what she enjoyed most in the world.

In the full-contact tournament, she had won three awards, each with cash prizes in excess of one million euros. This was in addition to her 15,000 euro-per-month salary from the corporation. Thanks to her gaming prowess, she had bought a penthouse apartment with a terrace and a magical view of Florence. A one-bedroom unit like hers was rare and overpriced, but the neighborhood was ideal.

Although she was proud of her achievements, she resented that her family was not—particularly her mother, who constantly questioned the source of her wealth. Her mom never stopped being suspicious of her money; in fact, she thought that Gina was the lover of some corrupt magnate . . . or worse! Of course, Gina's skill at the video game was not something that her mother could believe (or understand), but there was proof. Gina had not only shown her mother the game while she was playing but also the checks as they came in. How anyone got paid to play a video game was simply beyond her mother's understanding.

Her mother disliked her spending all those hours in front of a flat screen, but what was she supposed to do? Stop? The money was like nothing she had ever imagined as a child!

"Gina," she said every time the conversation turned to her career, "can you explain why they pay you? I don't understand. You are *playing a game*!"

"Mom, I've told you before. My games are being monitored by millions of users; what I do to survive in the game becomes the new programming. Basically, I am one of the few players who finds errors. I don't even program—I just play. The monitoring by the company is what counts."

"Okay, dear, but what happens if you stop being good? Will you lose this . . . *job*?"

"Just like any other job, Ma . . . it happens to everyone except politicians!"

Gina's mom couldn't help but laugh. And what she said was true; if Gina became bad or obsolete, she would need to find a new job. Gina's mother secretly wished for this to happen, even though the view of the river from the terrace was one of the prettiest sights she had ever seen.

After a long visit and coffee brewed in a Bialetti espresso machine, Gina began to grow tired of her mother. She politely asked her to leave in the frank way she had always spoken to her mother; it was calculated and reasoned. However, a twinkle in her eye revealed her desire to go back into the alluring world of Ultimatus.

"Goodbye, Mama," Gina said as she closed the beautiful door of the apartment.

Inside her bedroom, there was no light. The shutters hid the windows completely and only the light coming from the bedroom door splashed her shadow on the wall.

A switch was flicked and the noise of the hard drives in the gaming consoles began humming to life. The flat screen lit up, illuminating Gina as she removed her clothes and put on a tight one-piece Ultisuit. A long tether, like a bungee cord, was hooked to the back of the suit. That cord was also hooked to the wall about ten feet behind the large 60" monitor. Gina's body was perfectly formed, strong and lithe. Possessing the elasticity of a yoga master, Gina used custom foam cubes to find comfort in positions that other players only wished they could emulate.

With a smooth bend of her torso, and without bending her knees, Gina put on a pair of ankle bracelets. The arm bracelets connected the entire Ultisuit wirelessly to the computer with a single button. Small LED lights on her four extremities lit up at the same time. This Ultisuit was much more elegant and unobtrusive than the suit Noah had in his New York apartment. Gina's long rifle came next; she put it in a holder on her backpack. Then, Gina crouched in front of a small cabinet to pull out extra ammunition clips for her belt. Her superior equipment reflected her elite gaming status.

Her avatar immediately appeared on the large flat screen when she connected the last arm bracelet. Hand movements also moved her screen shots, and as soon as she could determine her location, Gina began to run. Running in place required precision and endurance, but her movements were perfectly matched by the on-screen figure that represented her. Her avatar was called BlingBlingBaby and had a svelte, yet curvaceous, figure— just like Gina's. In front of her, there were fallen trees from a recent storm; she leaped over them and continued toward her target.

On the way, she spotted a small object beneath a branch and stopped, her whole body dropping to the floor so that she could get closer to the object. With the end of her rifle, she moved some leaves and used the scope to aim at the branch. The zoomed-in area was visible on a small flat panel built into the gaming scope. A single rifle was lying on the ground ahead; she realized that a battle had recently transpired. She moved up slightly to see above the branch near her head; a shot cracked through the silence. Luckily, the bullet missed her by inches.

BlingBlingBaby looked to the right, left, and rear, gathering that the sniper was likely somewhere ahead. By the number of shots fired (four), she could tell that the player was a lonely beginner. Crawling away from her location, BlingBlingBaby placed a decoy from her virtual toolkit. As she moved away from the path to the thicker forest to her left, she kept glancing back at the decoy. It was made to keep moving up and down and looked like a head. The sniper continued taking potshots at the decoy, while she ran around the tree line to his flank. With a rapid change of weapons, her sniper rifle was suddenly aimed at her target. A young man at Scorsese-level or lower was in her crosshairs.

This will be a rude awakening, she thought.

She steadied her aim on his head when a different idea popped into her head.

Maybe I should test the program a bit.

Gina shot her opponent in the leg and then fired off a round into the side of his weapon. Sprinting toward him, she arrived at his side before he could even recover or stand.

"Are you hurt?" Gina asked through her microphone.
"What do you think? You bitch."

"Hey! Watch your mouth or I'll just shoot you on the spot."

Gina answered in perfect English, but with a silky Italian accent that made her voice sexy and engaging. She pressed her gun onto the sniper's temple. He moved his head to face her, and the barrel shifted to the center of his forehead. She wondered why the program didn't have facial expressions yet. Her opponent had a silly look on his face: somewhere between being wounded and stoic at the same time. Gina began speaking again.

"What's your name? Can you move your leg?"
"No. The shot disabled my leg components. I'm moving here at home, but the avatar isn't responding. I can move my arms though. See?"

The wounded sniper was gesturing with both arms raised; he even lifted a bit of debris from the floor and tried to chuck it at Gina.

"Easy there, cowboy. I'm trying to push how much the program can take. What did you say your name was?" Gina continued.
"I didn't."
"Where are you?"
"I'm not supposed to say . . . ."
"I know," Gina answered seductively. "Indulge me."

Gina backed up her sultry voice with the gun pressing a bit harder on the skull of her opponent. This was the longest she had ever taken to kill anyone in the game.

"I'm in Cincinnati. In the US."
"Yeah. I know where Cincinnati is."
"My name is . . . ."

Bang! A bullet left her rifle, and his avatar disappeared from the screen in an instant. Gina had lost her patience and the low-level player was unlikely to be any more help, but what he had contributed would be very valuable; now she knew that she could capture and interrogate other players, even torture them, if necessary.

Now I need to capture a Truffaut or a Spielberg. This technique should yield some interesting results in the upcoming tournament. I wonder where it will take place this time.

***

Maxine Novaes was one of the wealthiest heiresses in Brazil. Her son had been missing for more than a month, which was not only terrifying, but also unacceptable. Her mansion by the sea in Ferradura was surrounded by security guards, cameras, and high walls. She had all of the living spaces built on the second story, so the spectacular ocean view wouldn't be wasted behind the high walls that kept her estate safe. In a world where she was normally in complete control, she found herself in total lack of it. At that moment, she was waiting for the report from her private investigator, who was due to teleconference with her at any moment. Her estranged husband was unaware of these recent developments; Maxine didn't even bother to keep that cheating bastard in the loop about their missing son. Chico's father, Jose, had been dismissive of the entire situation, absolutely convinced that their son was out partying somewhere.

A lion thinks that all other animals are lions too. Maxine considered that old Latin saying, her mind circling the words of her ex, Jose.

The living room door opened and the housekeeper entered. Valentina appeared as if she had seen a ghost.

"Madame," she said quietly.

"Yes, Valentina. What is it?"

"It's monsieur."

"What did you say?"

"Mr. Santos is here," Valentina continued. "He is furious because I wouldn't let him in."

"Listen to me, Vale. Did he say anything about Chico?"

"Yes, he keeps saying, 'Chico this, Chico that.'"

Maxine rushed to the nearest phone and dialed the in-home number of the security guard at the gate.

"Mario? Mario! Let my husband in. Immediately."

Maxine put her distaste for her ex-husband to the side, hoping that Jose Santos might be aware of Chico's whereabouts.

Jose entered the living room dressed impeccably, looking like a human sculpture. He was a classic Latin playboy, living only for the moment and the next party. He was furious, obviously having just learned that Chico had been missing for weeks.

"Why? Why?" he continued demanding in louder and louder tones.

Maxine was speechless, instantly disarmed by his very presence. She very clearly still loved the man.

"Why what?"

"Why didn't you tell me?"

"I did tell you."

"But for weeks? This is not just a simple party. You never called back, so I assumed that he was back!"

"I'm sorry. I just . . . I can't even face you sometimes, not after what you did to me."

13

"You shouldn't take revenge on me by using Chico like this," Jose shouted.

"What? How can you even think such a thing!"

Beep. Beep, beep. The computer blared from across the room as they continued bickering with each other over the consequences of their hasty marriage too early in their lives.

"Wait!" Maxine screamed as she finally looked over at the sound of the computer. "The private investigator. Perhaps he found Chico."

Maxine woke the computer screen up and accepted the web invite to her scheduled teleconference session. The investigator was calling from a small hotel room in Marseille. The hotel room was decadently paneled, colored as though torn from a Matisse painting. Maxine and Jose were both looking at the tanned investigator. PI Moraleis recognized Jose immediately, as he had been the investigator who discovered Jose's cheating. He paused for a moment before beginning to speak.

"Hello, Maxine. Hello, Jose," PI Moraleis said. "I followed all of the leads to Marseille. The last flight taken by Chico led to this city. However, the trail quickly went cold. There were no records in any hotels, no credit card receipts . . . nothing. It is as if he landed and then disappeared. The only other things I gathered are strange comments relating to a video game called Oltimatus or Ultimatum . . . I'm not sure how to pronounce it."

"Ultimatus," Jose quickly clarified. "Ultimatus. At least, I think. Chico talked incessantly about that damn game. He used to play for hours. But why Marseille?"

"In this game, this Ultimatus, you apparently get an invitation to a tournament. People travel to fight in the game—in person. I don't know the rules, or where they play, but that's what I found out."

"But how can you be sure that this tournament was his reason for traveling?" Jose questioned warily.

"A bit of speculation and coincidence, actually. I met a CIA investigator who was asking a lot of the same questions as me. An American boy is also missing, under much the same circumstances. I learned that the company that owns the game is foreign, not only to us in Brazil, but also to the Americans. Everyone assumes that these games are American, but this one is not," Inspector Moraleis informed them ominously.

"Where is the game from?" Maxine asked.

"It has a corporate domicile in the Isle of Man."

"So do thousands, hell . . . millions of companies," Jose snidely retorted.

"The bigger problem is jurisdiction. There is no reason to even go to the Isle of Man. It's a dead end. The CIA is not welcome; the officer I met also told me that the offices of these companies are virtual. PO boxes exist at the headquarters, but no one mails anything anymore. Business is done online. You can open a company and run your business without ever meeting a single client in person; on top of that, the organizations and governments running these shell corporations won't allow any intrusion without a local court order. No crime has been committed on the Isle of Man. Essentially, no crime has taken place thus far—only a disappearance," Moraleis explained.

Maxine entered a state of semi-shock, and her normally pale skin faded further.

What can I do? Why would Chico go to Marseille without telling me? That damn game he always played . . . .

"Inspector Moraleis, I need you to investigate if a boat was used to take those kids to a larger boat. They must be in a yacht somewhere. Maybe this tournament is on the sea, or even on an island. What do you think?" Maxine rambled.

"I think I will need more money. There are hundreds of boats and dozens of yacht clubs. This will all take time and money."

"Inspector Moraleis, all I have is time and money. Keep working! Find him!"

Maxine stared at her husband with a helpless expression.

"One more question . . . do either of you know the name of Chico's . . . character in the Ultimatus game?" Inspector Morales asked, fumbling for the proper word.

Maxine and Jose's glances met guiltily—neither of them knew this potentially critical detail.

"Okay . . . why don't you ask around? His friends might know. Or maybe look in his computer logs . . . on his desk? We need to find out if he was at the tournament on the days immediately after his disappearance. However, without knowing his name, we can't know what actually happened."

"You mean this video game tournament might be responsible for his disappearance?" Jose asked.

"Exactly. From what I have heard in my research, this tournament has a full consequences clause It is an ironclad set of terms and conditions implying that anything that happens to the video personality on screen can possibly happen to the person at the tournament."

Maxine went from pale to transparent. She felt as if the remaining blood was draining from her brain. Before she could speak another word, she passed out on the plush sofa, her head tumbling to one side like a broken doll.

3

The CIA was always reluctant to begin investigations unless something was classified as "clear and present danger" or terrorism. The former director of the CIA had been unwilling to spend adequate resources on the Ultimatus case, but a new administration had taken control, which meant a new face at the top. This case only involved a handful of missing persons, so the issue could easily be passed off to local authorities, but there was a catch—Senator George was insisting that the agency pursue it. The senator from Rhode Island was personally involved because his nephew went missing after an unexpected trip to Marseille. What Senator George didn't know was that the agency had been involved long before his nephew had disappeared.

The new director, Robert Stewart, had headed up the operation before he ascended to his new position; the Internet was involved, and "cyber-anything" was a major priority in his vision for the agency's future. Somehow, this high-tech angle made him think that something interesting was going to arise. Robert considered implementing a new counter-cyberterrorism strategy that he had been developing for the past six months.

Now, under Stewart's new directive, the agency conceived a different plan and called for a computer expert to investigate the web domain of the alleged perpetrator. They also organized a team to perform any necessary aggressive action against the headquarters of the organization once it was found. According to the massive information-seeking initiative, it was discovered that the computer game allegedly *deleted* its players as they were killed. The last US player to die, Senator George's nephew, had apparently left some sort of electronic evidence, at least according to some of the deepest corners of the Darknet.

Director Stewart wanted to recruit a cyber expert for the job and was given plenty of options. Somehow, all roads had led to a young information technology guru that was gifted in gaming. His name was Simon Prince. Stewart ordered the new recruit to study the game and its possible connection to the missing US citizens.

Hard at work on this new lead, Simon received his first summons to the director's office. Robert began interviewing Simon in his office at Langley on a cold February afternoon. Robert was reading Simon's file when he came into the room and motioned for the young man to sit.

"You graduated third in computer science at Stanford . . . that's quite an academic achievement,"

Robert began.

Simon observed Stewart and remained silent, waiting for an actual question to be asked. Dr. Simon Prince was small in stature and geeky in a classic way, yet confident.

He belongs behind a computer screen, Robert thought.
"Your report on the game seems incomplete. What have you learned since then?"

Simon sat across from the imposing desk in a comfortable leather chair. The US flag hung limp behind Robert; the star portion crowned him in a comical way. If Simon squinted, he could almost picture the director of the CIA floating in space.
"Sir, we have almost reached the level of play that our missing gamer was at. I believe that this level not only requires better gear and a faster computer, but that I also must stop masking the IP address of our computer."
"What do you mean?" asked Robert.
"Well . . . we want to work at the Bureau itself to increase efficiency, so we've been suppressing the IP. That way, if the gaming company investigates us, they can't detect where we are playing from . . . Langley. However, when you graduate to Scorsese-level, a Trojan horse program is injected into the gamer's computer. I copied the code and analyzed it before continuing to play; an IP verification code is embedded. I have to restart the game at a real home to cover our IP address. I'll also need a faster computer, as well as various new tools that the game suggested," Simon explained.

Robert squinted and tried to conceal his lack of IT knowledge.
"I hope you aren't making all this up, Mr. Prince. All the equipment you buy has to be accounted for and returned to the bureau, right?"

"Of course, sir."

"Scorsese. What does 'Scorcese-level' mean?"

"It's a hierarchical level system. The best directors are at the top. The lesser known directors signal lower levels of skill."

"Who came up with this hierarchy?"

"Fellini. The creator and owner of Ultimatus," Simon explained.

"Fellini? Is that his real name?"

"It's unlikely that he was born with the same name as the greatest director in history."

"The greatest in history? I don't think I've ever seen a movie by that guy!" Robert joked.

"*Eight and a Half? La Dolce Vita?* Nothing? What about *Amarcord?*"

"Never seen them."

"Are you familiar with the term *paparazzi*?"

"Yes," Robert answered, confused.

"Well, that's the name of the photographer in *La Dolce Vita*," Simon told him, as though instructing a child on a basic concept.

"So it's an arbitrary choice, you mean."

"Absolutely, sir," Prince quickly agreed, not wanting to argue with the director. "Fellini's personal preference formed the hierarchy."

Robert paused, intrigued.

"Can you get me a list of this hierarchy?"

"You'll have it within the hour. Does this mean that you agree that I should continue from a private residence?" Simon asked. "With my assistant, Mark?"

"Why do you need him?"

"It's all in my report sir . . . ." There was an awkward pause before Simon explained. "Well . . . Mark is in pretty good shape, but I'm not. The game is intense . . . physically demanding. It would take me years . . . " he trailed off.

Director Stewart rang his intercom and asked his secretary to send Mark Sloan into the office.

"Why do you need Mark?" Simon asked.
"I ask the questions here, young man."

Mark entered the cavernous office of the Director of Central Intelligence and turned his head to take it all in. His expression betrayed his sense of awe. The walls were plastered with images of Robert with every president since Clinton!

This is amazing. Exactly what I imagined . . . only nicer, Mark thought.

Director Stewart pointed to a seat and proceeded to ask Mark everything that he had already went through with Simon.

"Mark. Is this game as physically demanding as Simon here seems to think?"
"More so, sir. I never imagined that a video game could be so . . . exhausting!" Mark answered honestly.
Simon interjected quickly. "I also keep Mark online longer than most players. The game records both time and calories burned It knows when you need food and water. You have to take care of your body, or else . . . ."
"Or else?" asked Robert, prompting over his pause.
"The machine shuts you down. Like death, practically. You start in a different server and play from a position of weakness, but if you survive, then you leap forward from one server to another, playing against better and better players. Once you clear a level, you enter the next one." Simon stopped to take a deep breath and have a sip of water.

"You can barely tell the story, let alone play the

game," Robert said, taking the opportunity to punctuate the lack of physical attributes the young genius had in an unexpected attempt to bring him down to earth.

Being smart is one thing, but it's certainly not everything.

Mark chipped in to back Simon up: "Basically, you stop and eat, but to do this safely, you need to hide to prevent being killed while in that downtime."

"Unless you clear a level," Simon interrupted him once more.

Director Stewart sensed a strange brotherly tension between the CIA agents. Ending the other person's sentences was not endearing or friendly; it was a challenge of expertise.

"Are you working well with each other?"

"Sure," Mark said quickly.

"Sure . . . sure," Simon agreed a bit more slowly. "I mean, Mark lacks the intuition about the mission, but I guess that's why he has me."

"I lack intuition? I'm the one who does the actual hard work. You just know how to pull a trigger," Simon shot back.

"Without me, you would still be a level-one player. Marshall-level . . . or maybe Badham."

"Shut it! Both of you. That's enough," Stewart broke up their bickering. "Why can't we just disable the servers?"

"Well, for one, we don't know where they are or how many there are. They could be anywhere in the world. Dozens of different countries," Simon added.

"Okay, then we stick to Plan A—get invited to this tournament. At the very least, do we know if the tournament is held where the servers are located?" Stewart asked.

"No," Simon admitted, frowning.

"Well, I'm sure Fellini will attend. And he is our target . . . right?" Mark offered.

"Or she . . . " Simon inserted.

"But until then, do we just continue this insanity? Do we have a choice?" Simon chirped, almost whiny. Mark and Director Stewart exchanged a glance, as if they both wanted the clever computer geek to just shut his mouth. Simon was displeased, but it had nothing to do with Mark or the conversation.

"No choice," Robert answered coldly. "You don't seem pleased, Simon."

"I'm not living in a secure location," Simon continued. "My cover can be blown so easily. Even the most basic tracking will lead here!"

"I never expected you to do this without full security. Damn, Simon, I want to wrap this up, and you're saying that you need more resources! This is the one case I don't have . . . ." Stewart shut his mouth mid-sentence.

Why let them know I am already on a limb with only a single senator in favor of this operation? It is going forward either way.

"Sir, if I may speak frankly, I think this is a big case. We're on to something here. I . . . as we reach higher levels, the company is bound to contact us. Chatter among players confirms that invitations to this year's tournament are imminent." Simon was visibly excited.

"That's true," Mark concurred, and then immediately shut his mouth, as if voting to stop arguing and continue the mission. In a way, he seemed eager to follow whatever decision got him back in the game fastest.

Dedicated to the job. Good for him, Robert thought to himself.

The phone rang and Robert gestured that he had to take the call. He motioned for Simon to approach, still listening intently on the phone. He wrote a quick note on his personal stationery and handed it to Simon. He turned to look at Mark and they both left the office, Robert motioning for them to get out. Simon walked down the wide corridor of the CIA, reading and smiling.

"What does it say?" Mark asked.

Simon continued strolling, saying nothing.

"What is it?"

Simon ignored Mark for a second time, and then he felt two massive arms seize him by the shoulders and lift him off the ground. Simon looked ridiculous as he continued trying to walk while his feet swung back and forth, not touching the floor.

"Fine, Jesus . . . put me down and I'll read it to you. Mark obediently lowered Simon back to earth: *"Get yourself a secure home and all the computer equipment you need. Report to me weekly. R.S."*

***

The offices of the Garda in Sligo, Ireland, had quite a different feel than other police stations in the world, primarily because the biggest problems were somehow related to being wildly intoxicated. There were no bars or bulletproof glass partitions; there weren't even metal cages, just old desks and computers from the last century. On this particular morning, DI Hughes sat at his desk, exhausted from many nights of scant sleep not because of working too hard, but because of his obsession with television. The countless streaming video options made his head spin. The ability to watch old programs beginning with the very first episode had drastically changed his habits; in short, he consumed way too much television.

Fatigued and bored, he was interrupted by an email that came as a welcome surprise.

Mary Peterson was at her home in Ballina, not far away, and had been waiting since earlier that morning for the police report on her missing son. She had seen the video game replay scene when her son's avatar had been playing in the tournament. Mary had found the YouTube kill-shot video of the exact moment when BPmyerson, had been eliminated from the tournament. The avatar had been fighting well and seemed to be winning, but a stray bullet had entered his head right above his ear and that was the end.

She was convinced that something terrible had happened to her son, but her husband, on the other hand, was convinced that Brendan was in no danger, simply up to his old shenanigans. Mary wasn't so sure; she sensed something sinister. DI Hughes called her and summoned her to the police station. The drive on the bluffs and down the valley roads to Sligo was gut-wrenching, so he was pleased when she agreed. Within a half hour, she pushed open the rusted blue steel door.

DI Hughes asked her to sit down and began reading from the paper in his hand.

"Interpol has now determined that there is no record of Brendan Peterson in any subsequent airport, train station, or bus terminal in the entire EU. Mr. Peterson is believed to be somewhere in the vicinity of Marseille, but if he travels by foot or by car, the system will not trigger a match until he uses his ID. He might also use a credit card, which would pin him down, but the last place one was used was at Dublin International Airport, where he paid for a one-way ticket to Marseille, connecting through Paris." Detective Inspector Hughes stopped reading.

"Mary," Hughes said, "Interpol has no way of finding him unless he surfaces with his identity or with a credit purchase. I, however, have been looking into the money, as you requested. You seem to think that he was making a lot of money with this game . . . job . . . whatever . . . ."

"He was always flush with cash. He even rebuilt our kitchen—all in cash."

"The thing is, his bank account is empty. You also said that he bought an apartment in town?"

"He claimed that he did," Mrs. Peterson said warily, not sure of anything anymore.

"Well, the bank had a note on it. It has to be paid soon. They'll be repossessing the apartment to pay the loan."

"Which bank?" Mary asked.

"A foreign bank. U.L.T.M. or something like that. Did you ever see any of the paychecks he received? Any other detail to go on?"

"No, it was all done online. Computers. I don't think physical mail ever came from that job. But he was making good money . . . great money. The company liked what he did for them, I guess. Just . . . playing."

Hughes laughed a little. "Sorry, Mary, I don't mean to laugh, but it sounds a bit fishy, you know? Playing a game and making that kind of money? A bit too good to be true, don't you think?"

4

Noah was a cool rider. Moving around Manhattan on a bicycle was both exhilarating and exhausting. He was an expert though, having weathered all types of biking situations in the past. His greatest fear, of course, was the unexpected opening of a car door as he whizzed by hundreds of parked cars, only inches away from moving ones on busy streets. This fear, and its severe consequences, was the greatest difference between life and the game. Playing offered the same level of high emotions that a dangerous life would contain, and in some ways, even more intense levels. These emotions seemed to soak into the players' subconscious minds and became addicting— irreplaceable.

Steam shot up from the street grates in Lower Manhattan; Noah could feel and smell the grit of NYC. No matter how modern this city seemed, the old steam-heated buildings from the turn of the nineteenth century reminded him of how much life actually differed from the game.

Smell was the only missing element in the game . . . .

Thank God, Noah thought.

At the East Village office of NY Fast Messengers, the mood was always tense and high-strung, making all the messengers feel guilty if they lingered. The job was about moving, not chitchat, but Noah was always ready and able to find someone to discuss Ultimatus with.

"I'm so close," Noah began telling his coworker, Jane.

"Oh yeah?" Jane said indifferently. She looked up and shrugged, reminding Noah that she had heard this before.

"No, really. This time, I know that I'm close."

"Well, I don't care. Those stupid video games took my brother away for hours every day, and for what? I only liked Minecraft. That was the only good one."

"You don't understand, Jane. If I graduate to Spielberg, then I'll start getting paid. I'll be able to quit this place. Ultimatus will finally be my *job.*"

"Listen, Noah, I don't want to sound like a buzzkill, but I'll believe it when I see your bank account. Until then, you better get off your pretty behind and deliver something. Get going!"

Noah left without saying goodbye, thinking how she would eat her words someday very soon. A loud twanging sound emanated from his bag, where he kept his cell phone. It was a text message from Ultimatus.

Turn on your game. You are officially a new employee of Ultimatus. Please do not let anyone know this until you read and understand the terms of your contract and click on the "Agree" button. You will receive your first payment after this process is completed. We expect you to begin dedicating a minimum of eight hours per day on the game. End of message.

Noah didn't say anything to Jane, nor did he pick up a batch of deliveries. He merely walked out of the office, unlocked his bike, and rode home, first going slow, still in shock, but then increasingly faster and faster. At home, he immediately went to his computer, opened the email waiting for him from Ultimatus, and slicked his finger to scroll through the terms and conditions in a split second.

Who actually reads these? What a waste of time . . . .

Then he strapped on his Ultisuit and mentally prepared himself for his first day of work at his new job.

5

Simon Prince was handsome in his own geeky style, but his love life was nonexistent due to his lack of self-esteem in the courtship arena. Much to his surprise, a woman, Patricia Knowles, had been corresponding with him, and their relationship was moving in the right direction; at least, it had been going well until the Ultimatus job fell in his lap. He had gone from being a cyber analyst to a field operative in less time than he had ever expected at the agency, but he had no way of telling her that.

Simon was sitting in a Starbucks in downtown D.C. Patricia sat across the table from him. She was pretty in a homely, yet austere, way and was dressed for jogging, with an iPod clipped on her sleeve. With a little work, she could have been considered attractive by many. Her facial expression was a mask of anger, seething with confusion and rage.

"I can't believe that you're saying this to me," she said, sputtering in fury.

"I'm sorry. It was just impossible for me to leave the office."

"What could possibly be so urgent that you can't see me on a Saturday night?"

"Pat . . . I'm all alone at the office. They're testing me to run the whole show. This is only temporary. I promise. I love you," Simon said.

"I'm not going to take any more of this from you. This weekend, we're going to my parents' place on the island. If you don't make it, then you can forget about seeing me again."

Simon liked Patricia well enough, but these tantrums and threats rubbed him the wrong way. He stood up and gave her a long, hard look, then kissed her forehead and walked out of the Starbucks to the busy sidewalk. She would understand once this mission was over and he could settle back into his normal routine . . . or maybe she wouldn't. He had never been very good at predicting or understanding women. He hailed a cab and gave the driver directions to go meet Mark.

Maybe she's just not "the one," Simon thought to himself.

Simon and Mark were working in a new apartment, disconnected from any possible CIA link. Simon had added a different frequency wireless earpiece to Mark's suit so that Mark could hear him in his left ear without disturbing the communication gear of the Ultimatus game. Simon was also hooked up to the output audio/video signal of Mark's monitors and had placed corresponding identical monitors behind these. In essence Simon was able to live in the Ultimatus experience just as much as Mark, but without the physical effort.

31

Ultimatus can never discover our identity—Slowpry's identity—or all this effort will be for nothing, Simon reminded himself regularly.

Slowpry was the name of their avatar. Earlier in the week they had received news that they would become paid gamers after leveling up to Spielberg, so Simon had been working Mark like a dog.

Mark's endurance was a true testament to what Navy Seals are actually capable of. The rifle in his arms was heavy, and he had to run in place, crouch, and fire hundreds of times, sending beads of sweat cascading down his body, even hitting the new computer screen panels, which were sixty inches in size. Slowpry had just conquered a level in the game after killing a few hundred high-level enemies. In reality, Mark was carrying a replica of a Russian AK-47 automatic rifle made of heavy-duty plastic.

These Russian rifles are way better than our M16s! They weigh less too.

Based on how well Slowpry moved and the speed of his kills, he deserved the upgrade. This time, the screen flashed a different reward. In the past, the game had allowed them to purchase and install new components of the game's plug-ins, but this time was different. Simon sensed that they were progressing toward their objective. The reward ceremony was different this time; it took place in a large stadium, where a full crowd applauded Slowpry, who stood in the center. From a side door, a stunning young woman dressed in a tight one-piece gym outfit moved toward Slowpry and kissed him long and hard on the lips. The gamer wrist and ankle guards sent a tingling sensation into Mark's most intimate nerves, and he flinched in false ecstasy.

"I could feel the kiss," Mark practically screamed even though his mouth hadn't been involved in the experience at all. "Wow!"

Simon couldn't help but roll his eyes in disbelief, although he had enjoyed the visual experience as much as Mark had. The programming in Ultimatus's advanced servers created such distinctive avatars that Mark felt the need to be playing all the time. It was almost as if that virtual reality might be a place where one could actually get to know someone.

In reality, Mark had no desire to start a serious relationship. Ever since his heart had been broken years earlier, he had shut that door, but the proximity to the opposite sex in the game was quite enjoyable. His love life has consisted of a series of girlfriends that all slightly resembled his high school sweetheart. He constantly looked for her in other women, which was his main problem. Mark was trying to replicate an impossible love. She had died in a car accident in her junior year, so the unpredictable and unexpected nature of life had been instilled in Mark when he was quite young. Mark still missed her all the time; she was the one person that really "got him." Losing your complementary piece in the puzzle of life was devastating. Her laughter at something he said or her willingness to play along with one of his silly jokes . . . were what he missed the most. The Navy was the only way to escape from that pain; sometimes, somewhere during the grueling physical routines of his training, he managed to forget her.

Slowpry was looking straight into the woman's eyes, and her face engulfed the flat screen before him until the camera zoomed into her pupil. In the darkness of the eyeball, at the back of the screen, sign was suspended upside down. It was reversed, as in a mirror, but Simon and Mark could both read it: *CLICK HERE TO DOWNLOAD*. An all too familiar download button . . . Mark clicked on it, instantly beginning their reward download. Again, no cost.

A quick three-scene summary from the end sequence of the movie *Close Encounters of the Third Kind* flashed across the screen. Simon recognized the classic film but couldn't seem to remember the director right away. He considered that the computer game must be paying royalties to the studio that owned the film, but he realized that those images and short scenes had been popping up throughout the game; *perhaps the corporation is violating copyright laws*. He made a note in his office pad for Director Stewart and continued observing. The humanoid-robot female in the film was the same person that virtually kissed Mark a moment ago. The computer began to flash a large, unmistakable message:

You are now entering Spielberg-level. You are now a part of a distinguished group of players. You will enjoy the following abilities. You will have greater strength in your body, meaning that it will be harder to fall to your death. Your skin will be tougher and you will be able to resist more punishment. All of the new commands are available for download; please print the full instruction set provided as a PDF. Also, you will find the new hardware list and the certificates to purchase these. Study these new features well, as you can lose these skills if you are careless.

Simon couldn't help but admit that this was cool. The creator of this game was a genius and potentially the mastermind behind a sinister plot. His evil genius status was yet to be determined. Simon gestured to Mark, who printed the instructions and certificates before logging out. Simon skimmed them quickly and found a new gun that they could purchase with an attached certificate; he would study more of the options later.

Simon picked up the certificate, folded it, and put it in his back pocket. "Let's go!"

"Wait a minute. I'm still in this Ultisuit thingamajig."

"Hurry up. I want to try this new stuff."

Mark rolled his eyes and disrobed, revealing his perfectly toned body.

"What a child," he said under his breath.

"I heard that," Simon barked.

Simon got dressed in street clothes and moved to the refrigerator in the adjoining kitchen. The apartment consisted of a living room, dining room, and kitchen area, as well as an attached bedroom with a full bath. The modern apartment certainly served the needs of the operation, although the gaming equipment took up over half the space. The windows had been tinted and neither of the residents ever opened them, giving a dark and seedy aura to the whole operation. Mark removed a can of soda from the fridge and drained it in two quick gulps.

"Are you done?" Simon said from the doorway.

"Oh, shut up. Just get in the car."

They left the apartment and simultaneously recoiled from the sunlight, blinded by the transition from their dark abode. Mark drove Simon's Honda CRV to the mall, because he hated Simon's driving, claiming that he always seemed distracted and never got places quickly enough. When they arrived at the game store, Mark leaped out of the car to buy the new gear, while Simon remained in the passenger seat. Simon worried that the corporation would be surveilling at the points of sale for their paid players; he didn't want to take any chances.

Mark emerged from the store a few minutes later and handed him the bag with the new gaming paraphernalia.

"Only $779. Not bad!" Simon exclaimed, clearly excited. "Back to the apartment!" Simon pointed forward as though Mark was his chauffeur.

Mark was ready to kill Simon by that point, but Simon was blissfully ignorant of his effect on his partner.

"You know what, Simon? Sometimes you really act like a rotten, spoiled child . . . . No, strike that. You *are* a spoiled child," Mark spat.
"Where does all this come from? You think that just because you're the body that sweats in the game, I'm not allowed to have some of the fun? I mean, you can't deny that these toys are cool. Right?"
"Yeah, I guess this stuff is cool to some people—people like you."

At the next stoplight, Mark grabbed the new toy weapon. It looked like a space gun straight out of *Blade Runner*. The weight was fantastic and the sensation was real, but real guns had been a part of Mark's training; these new toys were harmless, so he couldn't help but emit a cynical snort. Simon had already learned to hate that laugh. Mark chucked the gun back into Simon's lap and then gunned the gas pedal.

"Of all the jobs, of all the operatives, I get picked for the Toys "R" Us mission! Damn!"

They both laughed as the car sped down Canal Road toward the Georgetown area of Washington where Simon had rented the apartment. This mission was not only a physical challenge to Mark but also a mental one for Simon.

***

In the Rodriguez household, Mario Rodriguez wore the proverbial pants, but when it came to education, religion, and leisure for the children, Ligia took over. Ever since the iPhone had become popular in Mexico, she had been on a quest to disable and decommission any and all apps that kept the kids from their priorities. Ligia was so involved in this monitoring that she actually played with all the apps to make sure they were appropriate for her kids to use. *No* to Facebook, but *yes* to Instagram and Snapchat. *No* to Clash of Clans, but *yes* to Scrabble. Her criteria seemed irrational to her five children, ages twelve through eighteen, but Ultimatus seemed like the ideal solution to her biggest hatred of gaming—the lack of exercise.

When Ricardo Rodriguez took up Ultimatus, his body changed for the better. He became stronger, more fit, and he looked healthier. He also ate like a horse and had a growth spurt, shooting past Mario Jr., his older brother. He was almost taller than Mario Sr., his father! Ligia had no problems with Ultimatus. Yes, the equipment was expensive, but not any more expensive than a fancy dress for her or Maria. Plus, she had the money; Mario was working at Dillon Advertising as a creative director, and he seemed to be doing quite well. The fact that Mexico's economy was booming also helped.

However, their peaceful family balance had been disturbed when Ricardo disappeared. A few weeks after turning nineteen, he vanished without a trace. Of course, the family assumed that it was a kidnapping, but the police found that he had used his passport to travel to Europe. Mario and Ligia still suspected a kidnapping of some kind; Ricardo had never done this sort of thing, not without letting someone know. The police eventually stopped coming to her house to record phone calls from potential kidnappers. They were apologetic, but they explained that their resources were needed for real cases where there was at least some proof that a kidnapping had taken place. It simply wasn't a kidnapping in the eyes of the authorities. No ransom had been asked for. Nothing.

Why London? Ligia wondered which of her son's girlfriends had concocted this trip and seduced Ricardo into taking it. More importantly, she wondered what had stopped her dear son from making a simple phone call.

6

Gina was playing hard and fast. In the game, BlingBlingBaby was strolling through a beautiful train station modeled after Los Angeles Union Station. She was waiting for something, or someone, in the deserted train station. She sat on a wooden bench; nothing was moving. A fly entered the airspace near her. BlingBlingBaby remained motionless, but then quickly reached into the side pocket beneath her vest and grabbed a knife. She sliced through the air with an expert flick of her wrist. The sound of the fly had disappeared, because it was lying on the station floor, cut cleanly in two.

Speed seems enhanced on this level. Interesting. I wonder . . . Gina thought.

She stood up, still holding the knife, and hurled it at the train schedule board, which was made of wood. The knife thudded into the wood, buried deep but quivered slightly from the force of the impact. From right behind that spot, an avatar emerged, its hands held high in the air. Mark and Simon's Slowpry stood in the dusty darkness, trying to remain calm while interacting with this obvious killer.

"Sorry, but please don't kill me . . . ."
"Why shouldn't I?" BlingBlingBaby responded.
"I want to go to the tournament," Slowpry said.
"What's keeping you?"
"I haven't been invited."
"Well, I can't invite you."
"I know, but you're so beautiful, and you move so . . . so . . . " Mark blurted out, looking at Simon dumbly. Simon urged him on by moving his hands, trying to keep his attention on the screen.
"Flattery will get you nowhere. All I can tell you is that to get to the tournament, you will have to elude someone like me. However, you seem like easy pickings."

Without pausing for even a moment, Slowpry backflipped like a Cirque du Soleil acrobat and landed behind a train station chaise that looked like it came straight from the 1950s. He scanned the large hall for an exit and instantly decided on a low window facing an exterior patio. He took a knife from his belt and tossed it hard to his right. BlingBlingBaby turned at the noise and fired a shot in that direction, while Slowpry ran hard and jumped through the window. The tether on the suit worked perfectly; Mark was held back from hitting the large plasma screen. The avatar landed on the patio, and Slowpry ran in zigzags, avoiding possible gunfire, as though he had seen the devil herself.

If we get away from her, then we get the invite. Don't look back, just run, Mark encouraged himself silently.

After hearing the glass break, Gina clambered to another window and took aim at her quarry. Through her scope, Gina placed him directly in the crosshairs; she only had a few seconds to get him. She fired, but the bullet went wide as the avatar ducked and dodged to his left.

We'll meet again . . . perhaps in an environment where the stakes are even higher. Gina shook her head in amusement— *perhaps that opponent is worthy of the tournament.*

***

The hazy, hot, and humid summer weather of New York always pestered its citizens, but it was a particularly joyful day for Noah, which made him impervious to the weather. Noah gleefully walked out of Buenos Aires Restaurant on 6th and headed down the sidewalk toward Avenue A with a large GameStop shopping bag in his hand. He knew that he was about to experience one of the greatest sensations in his young life, short of sex . . . possibly. *Realistically, this will last a hell of a lot longer than sex.* This year's tournament experience would be quite different from his sedentary viewing in the past, just as it would be for millions of other Ultimatus players. It was a web event essential to any and all who wanted to succeed in the game. It was also a show packed with excitement, countless "instant replay highlight reel" kills, and an elaborate winner's ceremony.

This year, he would be *on* screens all over the world, rather than just watching one. He would be in the finals. He was determined.

As soon as I get back, I'm going to redesign my avatar. I'll make it distinctive. People watching should be able to recognize me.

Every year, the event happened in a new environment. The last contest had taken place in a virtual location that resembled the rocky terrain of Joshua Tree in California but redder somehow. It was a sort of Martian-like tundra where hiding was incredibly tough. Fortunately for the webcast viewers, a bird's-eye view was available on their computers. For obvious reasons, players in the tournament had no access to this. Discussions on countless chat streams and online rumors explained how finalists traveled to a private location so that they could play on an even basis. Noah was excited to go to the contest this year, which was, as always, rumored to be in a fantastic location.

The gaming plan and scenery were changed every year, which meant that the players and viewers were surprised with ever nicer and more complex locations. Whether or not the physical location for the tournament was in fact changed was not known to Noah or any other players. If anyone knew, they certainly weren't talking about it. He had never met any repeat finalists that knew that detail. Attending the event was the ideal opportunity to find out, which obviously excited him. Back in front of his computer, he began by adding a red helmet that had an attachment of red Mohawk-hair on top. Then he immediately removed it and shook his head.

It would be stupid to call so much attention to myself. I'd get taken out within a minute. No wonder the winners are always dressed as plainly as possible. Urban camouflage.

He began to style himself in a more subtle, under-the-radar way, which got him on the right path. For the first time, he was thinking like a professional player, more conniving and astute, rather than flashy and dramatic like normal everyday players. He would become a killing machine—a brilliant, strategic psychopath. He put his avatar in dark clothing, as indistinct and unmemorable as possible. As a newly advanced player in the game, he yearned to try out his newest acquisition.

In the shopping bag was an updated version of the Ultisuit that had cost nearly $700. He had to admit, the purchase felt much more gratifying when he used the money that he had received from the Ultimatus Corporation itself. Not needing any more income than the company check from Ultimatus was a development in his life that he could definitely get used to.

I can't believe I'm getting paid for this, Noah thought as he read the installation instructions.

Plenty of rich kids owned this gear because they acquired all the Ultimatus toys that they could get their parents to buy, but they used the elite items with limited capabilities since they couldn't buy the computer programming updates needed to activate them. Only skill unlocked those attributes.

In a frantic matter of minutes, Noah had installed the tether hook with its two long lag screws into a wood stud behind the wall plaster, as the instructions had directed. He measured the cord three times to make sure it had enough give. Noah was strangely skillful at construction and putting things together; he had grown up watching his father fix everything around the house. He tested this new tether feature; it allowed his avatar to jump forward much farther than before. The idea of playing in this new suit, with these new abilities, was exhilarating. Being outfitted in the latest gear made his expectations soar in terms of getting the invite. He found a new objective written on a wall outside the villa. The instructions were clear:

You must not be wounded, not even a cut.

You must kill a minimum of 20 players.
You must drive the speedboat to Red Island.
If you can elude the guards and reach the center plaza of the island castle, you will be attending the 5th Annual Ultimatus Tournament.
You will not receive these instructions again.

Noah quickly wrote them down on a pad that he kept near his game set-up, but he didn't need to. He wouldn't forget those five sentences for as long as he lived.

This is it. No turning back.

Noah88 noted the lack of enemies in this new level. The streets of the nearby urban area were deserted, like a post-nuclear world. Buildings stood empty, and graffiti cobwebbed their walls and windows. Noah was both mesmerized and intimidated but quickly realized that he would be easy pickings unless he came up with a strategy—fast.

Rule Number One: High ground. Now!

The tallest building in the vicinity was three stories high, and he immediately made that his priority. However, this was probably not a unique idea, and hastily running into a bloodbath would not be to his advantage.

Rule Number Two: Patience.

Noah88 crouched near a trash container and angled himself to make sure that no one could approach him from behind. He surveyed the entire area but saw no movement. From this location, the three-story building with an old-fashioned water tank on top was visible. He aimed his sniper gun at the building.

In his apartment, Noah was crouching in a sideways tiger pose with the weight of his gun on his shoulder. He moved a heavy exercise ball to allow his cantilevered weight to rest.

Rule Number Three: When possible, get comfortable.

Above the tower, a slight flicker of light flashed. Noah88 aimed at the wooden structure exactly where the body of his opponent would be lying based on that glimmer of movement. He was counting on his high-caliber round to pierce the wood. He squeezed the trigger, and the thud of a kill sounded off and registered on his kill line. *Nineteen to go.* He had the option of sniping from the tower, but that hadn't worked for the last player. He also couldn't be sure if he had killed a green player or a high-level competitor. If wounded, the player might be cooperative. Noah88 glanced around the space, checked his angles for other snipers, and ran quickly to the entrance of the building.

Inside the building, he noticed that it had been designed as an abandoned hotel. Seedy and cheap, the former establishment had a front desk installed behind bulletproof glass. Instead of going upstairs immediately, he moved behind the counter, leaving the small open space in the bulletproof glass directly in front of him. He placed his rifle through the hole and positioned himself comfortably. No movement . . . not a muscle, not even a smile. He assumed that someone would walk in and his second kill would be guaranteed by the safety of the glass. Once he took this kill, he decided that he would go to the third floor.

A good ten minutes later, practically an eternity in a video game, the front door slammed open and a fast-moving player rolled in. Noah's instinctive first shot

45

missed him, and this new avatar began shooting at him. The glass worked perfectly, ricocheting the man's bullets; somewhere in the back and forth of the shooting, Noah's opponent caught a bullet with his forehead, stopping him dead in his tracks. Before the player even fell to the ground, Noah88 was headed upstairs. A second kill would attract unwanted attention to his position and his skill. These players were top-notch tournament seekers; their positioning, their movements, and their instincts were all excellent.

Noah88 reached the top floor and found the avatar that had received his earlier shot on the rooftop. Wounded and far from his rifle, the gamer saw Noah88 approach him with his handgun drawn. He was a dying man with black skin, black clothing, and red splotches of blood across his abdomen.

"Don't move," Noah88 said.
"I can't. I'm paralyzed. I'm dying," he choked out the words.
"Well, before you go, tell me something. Are you trying to get to Red Island?"

He nodded. In what seemed to be virtual pain, his avatar began to die and then froze in place. The body did not disappear as it usually did in lower levels, which was an interesting difference that would have to be considered. Kills remained behind, which complicated matters. The body in the lobby would be seen, and so would this one. Noah grabbed the body and pushed it off the parapet wall onto the roof of the two-story building below, hoping to keep it somewhat hidden

Noah was clearly playing against great players that were in peak shape. This level had no easy-to-kill fourteen-year-olds still learning to use their controllers. *Eighteen kills to go* . . . He scaled the water tower in order to survey the map and hopefully find a body of water. Then he would get away from this building. Too many shots had been fired here, and they would inevitably attract more players.

From high on the water tower he surveyed the whole map, which was a visual disappointment, peppered with stark, barren areas, like abandoned parking lots, and plenty of red dust. A green mountain in the distance lay motionless on the horizon.

Any water must be near that green mountain . . . north, maybe northwest, of here, Noah thought.

Noah hurried to the stairs on the side of the water tower and slid down the sides, not taking the time to step down all the rungs. The sound of a bullet sliced the air and clanged off the metal tower.

Definitely time to go.

To escape unscathed, he would need to leave a different way than he came in. The stair access that he used to get to this roof needed to be shut. He locked the entry with a spare piece of metal wire lying nearby. He then ran in the direction of the next-lowest building and gauged the jump it would require. It was his first real use of the bungee cord tied to his back and he hoped that he would instinctively figure it out. He ran quickly toward the edge and dove head-first toward his screen. The cord allowed him to throw himself forward, but then tugged him back onto his feet. His avatar, however, soared forward and landed on the next rooftop. He didn't stay to enjoy the moment; instead, he kept running. He knew what direction to go, and he was determined to kill anyone that got in his way.

Breaking down the door to the roof with his

shoulder, Slowpry (Mark with Simon in his ear) emerged on the empty rooftop. In the distance, a body sprinted across the roof of the fourth building over. He aimed quickly, but the small figure and its speed meant that the bullet would be wasted, only serving to draw attention to himself. He decided to travel up the water tower to survey the landscape. Moments later, he came to a similar conclusion as Noah.

North . . . maybe northwest, Simon decided and set off.

7

Eric Bergstrom had been the Chief Detective
Inspector of the Stockholm Police Department for more
years than his marriage had lasted, twenty-three to twenty.
One of his most frustrating investigations involved the
disappearance of three Swedish citizens over a period of
three years; all that they had in common was an invitation
to the Ultimatus final competition.

He decided to find the location of this tournament
and formed a staff of three inspectors for the
investigation. This year, he would do things better and
gain the necessary advantage he needed to succeed.
Ingeborg Larsson, his assistant, had worked undercover
for months and had found a player in a hip Stockholm bar
that seemed to have the fan status of a rock star. This
player had a body fit enough for the Swedish Special
Forces, and Ingeborg had met him and allowed him to
ramble about his "job" playing the game. Some drinks
later, she discovered that he had a guaranteed entry pass to
the tournament.

Eric wanted Ingeborg to ensure that this guy would attend the tournament before spending the precious budget for equipment. Losses were not an option. He pushed her just short of ordering her to sleep with him, even hinting that she should move into his loft if possible. She wanted to refuse on basic principle, and if the player had been your typical computer nerd, then there would have been no way in hell that she'd be getting into that situation. However, Stellan was handsome and fit, which made her perceive the job from a very different angle.

She accepted his offers of drinks, meals, and eventual lodging, teasing Stellan for information about the tournament by promising herself to him. The worst-case scenario? Falling for Stellan Boström. However, that silly risk existed in any situation and at any time; plus, Ingeborg had a thick skin when it came to love. She had become a police officer to add an extra buffer between her and any potential suitors. Love and Ingeborg had parted ways long ago.

Ingeborg's familiarity with Ultimatus began early, when she and her younger brother had played in the years before he left for college. She liked the game, but as many females complained, the excessive violence and the demands once a player became serious about the game put her off. When a game took precedence over checking Instagram or answering the phone—that was the point where she lost interest, which was true of many people. Ingeborg also drew the line at those silly hand straps.

Going to Stellan's flat for the first time showed her the level of professionalism the top Ultimatus players achieved. Stellan spoke of the game corporation like Apple employees speak of their elite company. One important difference between these levels of adoration was that no one knew the name of Ultimatus's creator. "Fellini" was an avatar name. Or was it a level? No one knew for sure, but Fellini was the only name for "him." Everyone used the name. After two or three weeks of working on, and sleeping with, Stellan, Ingeborg had heard more about Firemist1 and Fellini than she had ever expected.

Eric continued pressuring Ingeborg to find out dates, but Stellan simply did not have them. Ingeborg told Eric that the invite should appear at some point during the summer, probably in August. Stellan had already told her that he would leave the minute he received the invitation. Therefore, Eric ordered her to place the tracking GPS sooner rather than later. Ingeborg was obviously in danger, and the chance of missing the window of opportunity for another year meant that the loss of a GPS transmitter would have to be risked. He told Ingeborg to find out what Stellan's favorite item of clothing was or whether he had some sort of lucky charm.

Ingeborg eventually predicted that Stellan's favorite belt would be ideal. She had never seen him out of his flat without it.

She still had to find the right moment to insert the wafer-thin GPS tracker in the belt. In her jacket, she had leather tools to cut and sew the leather back in place. One particular night, she waited for him to exit his gaming room and sat on his living room couch wearing nothing but her jacket. He left his gaming space exhausted, sweating, and wearing only shorts. The difference between that night and hundreds of others playing the game was Ingeborg's presence on his couch.

They fell into each other's arms and a half hour later, Stellan was sleeping like a log. Ingeborg quietly refashioned the belt with the GPS device, worried sick that her handiwork would be apparent. Tying the final knot in the belt was the hardest part; she tried to remember the detailed instructions that the police tailor had given her. Her work looked a bit suspicious to her, but you would probably need to be searching for it to notice.

I certainly hope he wears this to the tournament.

Inspector Bergstrom lacked the exact details of how the tournament players were selected, but his gut told him that there must be a hierarchy. Some players were granted automatic admission, whereas others needed to prove themselves to get in. Through chat rooms and various forms of alternative research, Eric found out that Stellan's Firemist1 was one of the best avatars in the world. He had been an excellent player for Ingeborg to attach herself to. Firemist1 had attended all four tournaments and had survived each one. He had spoken with Fellini and had possibly even done so in person. Ingeborg had heard this from Stellan as well, but she still wasn't sure how it would all play out.

Eric, however, thought that Stellan was the key to the whole operation.

On August 8, at noon, Ingeborg received a text from Stellan:

Got the invite. Gotta go. Will be in touch when I come back.

Ingeborg panicked and ran to Eric's office.

"Detective Inspector! Look!" She began speaking as she stormed into his office, but instantly realized that he was on the phone.

Her face, however, commanded his attention, and Eric quickly hung up. She quickly circled the desk and handed him the phone with the open text.

"What should I answer?"
"Ask him about where he's going. And tell him you'd like to see him off."

Ingeborg nodded and set her fingers to typing:

But I can't let you go without a goodbye. Where are you going? Let me at least see you off.
I am on my way to Arlanda Airport. My plane leaves in 2 hours. Stellan texted.
I can meet you. What airline?
British Airways.
OK, puss puss.

"Only one flight leaves in two hours with British; he must be on his way to London," Eric concluded. "Ask him."

"He might get suspicious," Ingeborg cautioned. "I better just get over to Arlanda and see him off. That way we'll be sure."

"Go."

Ingeborg arrived at Stockholm Arlanda Airport before Stellan. Unaware of this, she worried that Stellan had already passed through security, so she called him on his cell. Stellan glanced at his vibrating phone as he entered the automatic parting doors of the airport. He read her name on the iPhone screen, and before he could answer, the face to whom the name belonged appeared before his eyes. She was truly beautiful; this would be his first airport goodbye with a woman that was not his mother. Ingeborg ran toward him and they embraced. In the middle of the kiss, she slipped her hands under his coat to make sure that he was wearing the belt.

Good, he brought it, Ingeborg thought, despite feeling

53

guilty; she had grown quite fond of this devilish, handsome gamer.

Eric Bergstrom needed to follow the GPS. Limits to the signal strength, as well as human error, pressed him to action. If Stellan boarded a long flight, they might not be able to track him when he arrived, as he would likely be out of range. Ingeborg had to find out Stellan's definite destination, and Eric needed to organize transportation to follow this key player.

Ingeborg excelled in her duties and stuck with Stellan all the way to security, where the guards informed her that she could not continue. She held him back for another few minutes and continued drawing out their goodbye. Throughout this process of affection and farewell, she had managed to see his ticket. She had confirmed his destination: London's Heathrow Airport.

Eric's hunch was right.

She needed to convey this information to Eric but had to wait for Stellan to pass through security. As they waved a final goodbye and he disappeared around a corner, heading for his gate, she pulled her phone from her coat pocket and texted Eric.

To Heathrow. Flight 853. Leaves in 1 hour.

Eric had to scramble. London being the destination was both good and bad. It was good because he had a chance to board the same plane that Stellan was taking. It was bad because London Heathrow was one of the largest airports in the world, from which Stellan could fly to hundreds of far more remote locations. He made a call to delay the plane until he and William Ramel, his trusted tech genius, could arrive and board the flight.

Ingeborg arranged the delay with airport security so that it would happen before passengers moved into the plane. Eric did not want to be seen boarding last, so that everyone on the plane saw him and resented his tardiness as the cause of the delay. He sped through Stockholm like a madman, employing his rarely used siren on the roof for the entire journey. William was fiddling with an iPad, tracking the blue dot of Stellan's belt with the GPS program on the screen.

They arrived and were greeted at the airport by Ingeborg. She handed them their tickets and half-heartedly wished them luck. Once they grabbed their gear, she took Eric's keys and drove back to the station in his BMW 3 Series.

Saying goodbye to Stellan felt awful. *What if. . . .*

She tried to stop thinking of Stellan's possible disappearance and had to constantly remind herself that she was, in fact, working undercover. *This is getting complicated . . . .*

Eric and William managed to get on the same plane as Stellan, which meant that the GPS would be invaluable. Stellan went to the baggage claim to see if he could spot any other players. Sometimes, the game began long before you put on the Ultisuit.

For the first time in his life, in London of all places, Stellan realized that his English sounded quite funky. He spoke like a true Swede, with a heavy accent, so he kept his speech to a minimum. Once he retrieved his bag from the baggage claim area, he strolled to the nearest taxi stand. Eric noted that Stellan had not checked his phone or come into contact with anyone. William blathered on about needing to plug in as much as possible, but Eric was more worried about finding their contacts in London.

"Will, get the bags," Eric said sternly. "I need to go outside and find Peter."

Eric went through the sliding doors that welcomed in a palpable wave of damp British air. His eyes searched for his English contact from MI6. Peter Lang stood outside a four-door Maserati, leaning casually on the hood, sporting a stylish pair of sunglasses and a smug look.

What in the world? Eric was shocked, but he couldn't help but smile and shake his head in disbelief.

"They must be paying pretty well over here in England," Eric joked and motioned to the beautiful car behind Peter.

"A temporary situation, my friend," Peter explained. "I'm in the middle of a high-profile case, and I need to play the part. Besides, this Maserati is an old drug dealer's vehicle, decommissioned by her Majesty for our personal use."

"Right, but I need to follow someone without drawing attention on every street. A Maserati isn't exactly what I was counting on," Eric continued.

"Don't worry, my boy, this is an old model; plus, with this metallic brown, people hardly notice," Peter assured him.

"Wait here, I'll get the baggage—and William. Just stay here. We're going to follow him with our GPS, so be ready."

"Brilliant, will do," Peter confirmed.

Stellan flagged down a car service and proceeded into a drawn-out discussion with the driver, who seemed reluctant. However, he eventually agreed to drive this Swede when shown a couple of crisp 100-euro notes. Neither Peter nor Eric saw Stellan leave the airport and head toward the highway. Almost ten minutes later, once

William had finally collected his equipment from baggage claim, they found themselves in the back of the Maserati, screaming and shouting that they were miles behind. That was the beauty of GPS, however, and it worked beautifully; they followed the taxi from a distance of two miles without a single glitch.

The road to Dover was a fast drive down a primarily straight freeway, and the entire trip lasted just over an hour and a half. Eric was pleased that Stellan had not taken another flight from within Heathrow. England was relatively close to Sweden, given the other possibilities for transportation hubs worldwide. Eric assumed that the tournament was being held in England and considered enlightening his colleagues at Interpol. That was the sort of strategy that would pay dividends in the future; he was already expecting to be promoted if he stopped or solved the Ultimatus disappearances.

William was noisily eating crisps in the backseat, and the crunching sounds coming from the backseat seemed to bother Peter.

"Here now, boy, stop eating in the Maserati!" Peter suddenly scolded Will.

"Hey, Peter. Are you okay?" Eric asked. He had known Peter for many years, and that was a strangely sharp response to a colleague.

"No. I'm not," Peter said coldly.

"What's going on?" Eric asked, seeing a chance to step in and advise an old friend.

"I'm not happy about being on a wild goose chase right now. I'm working on another case and am painfully close to nailing the bastard," Peter explained.

"I'm sorry if we inconvenienced you, Peter. I don't think this will last too long. Nice and simple."

"Hey. Guys," William mumbled, potato chips still in his mouth.

"You can go back if you want, Peter. We can rent a car as soon as . . . ."

"Hey! Guys!"

"What?" Peter and Eric responded in unison.

"Stellan stopped right ahead."

"Careful, Peter; we don't want to spook him."

"There," William said, pointing at a lone car parked on the grounds of a large seaside hotel.

The Best Western Dover Marina Hotel was a long, narrow building with a beautiful facade facing the ocean— a few minutes from the famous white cliffs. Stellan paid his cab and entered the lobby, where he recovered his pre-registered, all-expenses-paid keycard. He declined the help of the attending bellboy.

"I can manage," he said to the bellboy, but still extended his hand and gave him a 2-euro coin. "Thanks anyways."

"Thank you, sir."

Do call me sir . . . Stellan thought, laughing inwardly.

Stellan's youth made him feel uncomfortable when he was called *Sir,* but it also amused him. In his room, Stellan found a mailer pouch with an instructional letter on top. He didn't have to read the note; he had done this before. As soon as the last text instructions arrived, he would place his cell phone in the pouch and leave it for the corporation staff to return once the tournament ended.

The text will arrive in minutes or days. There's never any way to know, Stellan mused.

Stellan had to wait for an undisclosed amount of time before his next text message instructions arrived, so he got comfortable in his room. He had attended tournaments in the past and remembered that anticipation could be a much more dangerous killer, so he decided to indulge during the waiting period. The corporation kept close tabs on expenses, so he assumed that he would receive the text at some point the following day. He drew a bath, took off all his clothes, ordered room service, and jumped into the tub.

Meanwhile, Chief Detective Inspector Eric Bergstrom had been scrambling to find accommodations in Dover. The Marina Hotel was fully booked, according to the front desk manager, and they needed to be nearby. Peter didn't let rejection from the manager intimidate him. He explained who he was, dramatically hinted at the nature of their mission, and had the keys to a single room with two beds at the Marina Hotel within five minutes. Extra rooms were always available, as hotels always kept some in reserve for special guests—you just needed to know how to get them. He could have gotten another, but Peter was eager to get back to his own case, and the lack of rooms was a perfect excuse for him to leave them.

"You can rent a car here at the hotel," Peter explained.

"Great. But would you mind waiting until we have the vehicle? Then you can be on your way, Peter. I don't want Stellan to start moving before we can follow him. That could happen at any moment; this whole thing seems to be very . . . spontaneous," Eric said.

"Of course, Eric, I wouldn't do that. Your options are Avis or Europcar," Peter told them, pointing toward the two lobby signs.

"Europcar, obviously. Our budget is already off the charts!"

Eric and William settled in a small room once they had a car ready at the car park. The blue dot of Stellan remained in the same building they were in, so they went to have dinner at the hotel. Famished, they ate heartily, and although the hotel food was terrible, their hunger seasoned the meal toward edibility.

I miss Swedish meatballs, Eric thought, taking his mind off the case for a few precious minutes. He had been trying to ignore William, who talked constantly, but had thus far failed to wean out his irritating voice.

Eric prepared William for what would likely be a surveillance evening. Until 2 a.m., William would have to stay up monitoring the GPS. William would then wake Eric up and switch roles. William agreed, but was disappointed that the TV set was off-limits; Eric said that it would keep him awake. It was only 8 p.m. when Eric felt ready to crash. They parted ways in the lobby, William deciding to avoid the boredom of the room for a while longer and pleased that the iPad allowed him some mobility.

Police work can be so boring, William thought, laughing as he remembered his dreams of constant car chases.

He sat on the comfortable lobby couch and opened a new game of Scrabble on the device, making sure that the GPS screen was only one tab over. He let his eyes drift and began to people watch. A bride walked back from her reception, completely plastered. A couple walked hand in hand, occasionally looking into one another's faces and saying nothing—the silence of love.

Unfortunately, as the investigation was not proceeding in Sweden, they lacked access to a surveillance team and a hallway detail to control movement and identify possible leads based on contact with Stellan. A single lead could open the whole investigation up, but for now, being in the same hotel as that blue dot was the best they had.

At 2 a.m., William woke Eric up and crashed to

sleep, only to be woken four hours later when Eric decided to start their day of work. William dressed and readied himself as if exhumed from a grave; that short stretch of sleep was unusual for the tech prodigy. However, William knew that he needed to pay his dues in the department—complaining would get him nowhere.

As the two officers readied themselves for the day, Stellan dreamt of an endless swimming pool and a handful of cocktails. It was a peaceful, restful sleep, the slumber of a man without a care in the world. In Stellan's mind, all the security and secrecy of Ultimatus was part of the corporation's plan to avoid groupies and maintain the tournament's mysterious quality. The best explanation for all these short trips, text messages, and split-second movements was protecting the secrecy of the location, which changed every year. You couldn't afford to question Fellini if you wanted to attend the tournament. Even if you had issues to raise with the head of Ultimatus, a complaint box didn't exist.

"We've got movement!" William said.
"Let's go." Eric leaped up from his chair, grabbing the car keys and his gun.

Stellan had been texted to catch a cab and drive to a specific location. The Marina Hotel always had empty cabs waiting outside; Stellan quickly slid into one and was driven away. William and Eric followed, approximately five minutes behind.

Stellan arrived at an empty field above the Dover Cliffs, where five other players were similarly arriving in their own cabs. They all looked at one another, while also following the subtle hand signals from the crew of six other men, all dressed in black.

The precise arrival of all six players was yet another

example of Fellini's timing—it had been impeccable.

Eric and William were close, but had not topped the final few hills. They saw that the blue dot had stopped moving, so they slowed their pace. Before they reached Stellan's location, he was swept by a corporation worker with a wand. The apparatus beeped the moment it reached Stellan's belt.

"Take off the belt."
"But it's my favorite belt, man." Stellan said, frustrated.
"Off. Now! Or you can call another taxi home."
"Jesus. Okay . . . " Stellan answered with a sharp tone but unbuckled the belt obediently.

The worker took the belt, turned away, and swept a smaller wand over the belt, locating the exact spot where Ingeborg had inserted the GPS tracker. He took a knife, cut the seam, removed the wafer, and threw the device on the grass, where he crushed it beneath his boot. He turned around and handed Stellan his "cleaned" belt.

"Thanks. It's my favorite belt," Stellan said.
"Yeah. You mentioned that. Now go to the instructor up ahead," the stern employee barked at him. As Stellan stepped forward, the worker made a note on a small device he had in his chest pocket.

The other workers were opening the wings of six large hang gliders. Stellan approached the man opening the glider nearest him and began to help. He held a wing open as the snaps and safeties were inserted in their proper places. Within a few minutes, the six players were paired up with the six workers; they were harnessed together and began walking, then jogging, then sprinting toward the edge of the cliffs. When Stellan's feet left the ground, his stomach admittedly plunged. The whole set-up and takeoff lasted four or five minutes. All twelve people were now moving straight over the ocean and deep into the fog that hung up ahead. They left nothing behind, save Stellan's GPS wafer, which actually belonged to the Swedish Police. The other five players had been clean upon arrival.

Eric and William's iPad showed that the blue dot had still not moved from the edge of the map. Eric stopped the car and decided to approach slowly. He didn't want to rush in and risk the whole operation, but he didn't see how the tournament could possibly be held there.

"What's there? Where the dot is?" Eric asked.
"That is there," William answered, pointing at the end of the map.
"Where?"
"There." William zoomed in to the field next to the Dover Cliffs; there were no buildings nearby.
"Are you fucking kidding? Let's go!" Eric commanded William, a sickening wave washing over his entire system.

William drove the next mile and then stopped. He got out of the car and followed the GPS signal in the deepest zoom it could go. He closed the gap and then saw that he had passed the dot.

"We passed the signal."
"Can't be, Will. Are you saying that GPS tracker was broken?"

William turned around, ignoring Eric's question. He stepped cautiously, and when the blue dot aligned, he looked up at the sky and then down at the ground. Right in front of his shoe, a Swedish police GPS tracker, model AD-0363, sat half-submerged in mud.

"Here it is," William said with a mixture of relief and disappointment.

"Don't touch it!" Eric snapped.

Eric donned a latex glove and picked up the tracker, then used the same glove as a carrying device by flipping it off his hand and over the wafer. He then surveyed the entire hilltop and took pictures of the tracks left by the players. Eric searched so intently that he even laid on his stomach at the edge to see if the players had scaled down. William begged Eric not to get so close, as the fall would certainly be fatal, but Eric was possessed by something that William could not understand.

AHHHHhhhhh—SO CLOSE and still . . . nothing, Eric thought.

Eric had been dealt another blow to his ego by none other than Fellini himself! Back in the Stockholm Head Office, he would learn that the only DNA on the tracker belonged to Ingeborg.

Dead end. Again.

8

Slowpry had been summoned to the "invitation to the tournament" computer server in the same way as Noah88, whom he had just spotted from behind. He was determined to find the boat to Red Island and speculated that the direction the mystery player took was the correct route. Two problems immediately arose in his mind. The first was that if he followed that player, there was the chance of being killed by Noah88 himself. The second was that he needed twenty kills to "advance."

"Stay here. Hide and wait," Simon warned him through the earpiece.

"Why?"

"I think the direction that kid ran in is right, but this rooftop is the best place to see this space. Someone is bound to come up those stairs. We can at least get our first kill."

As Simon spoke, Slowpry was already moving to crouch behind a large exhaust fan shaped like a mushroom. The door was almost directly in front of him and half-closed, the opening not visible to Slowpry. Whoever showed up would most likely throw the door open and come out shooting.

Slowpry waited patiently. As expected, a force moved the door open. Slowpry remained in place as bullets flew in every direction, scattering sparks in a wide arc in front of the door. A minute or so later, a body ascended the water tower stairs.

Slowpry's first kill shot was cowardly, from behind, but it still counted.

Nineteen to go.

Simon had assumed that there would be a larger crowd of players, considering that twenty kills for all thirty finalists meant at least six hundred players. Mathematics suggested that there should be even more players, but the experience had thus far been barren. Mark was not worried. He had been to the Middle East, where thousands of people lived in crowded streets, but as soon as shots were heard, any bustling intersection could turn into a desert in seconds. He knew that humans lurked in the shadows.

Every year, ten champion players were invited to return to the tournament, so the total number of new finalists was twenty. Simon had miscalculated by a third. Four hundred players in the whole world had been invited—only twenty would attend. Contestants like Gina and Stellan were the cream of the crop, so they did not need to participate in the tournament invitation server. Of course, once in the final tournament, any new player of the twenty could join the ranks of the top ten if they performed well. These winners yielded the bulk of the statistics and the glory that made Ultimatus not only the most popular, but also the most lucrative, game in the world.

Mark was getting worried. Any kill would bring attention to a given area. The next player might be more thorough and not overlook the fan. Staying in that spot seemed like a high-risk move. Slowpry moved in the same direction he had seen Noah88 head in. He jumped boldly, using the tether as though it was second nature. Unbeknownst to him, Mark's physical skills were superior to most players. He leaped off the last building and moved into the forest behind the structure as quickly as he could.

This spot is ripe for another kill . . . Mark thought for a moment, covering the microphone on his headset with his palm.

"Simon, do you think we should wait for the next guy?" Mark said.

"I'm worried that whoever gets here might be good, but you're right . . . we could hide and get one more kill," Simon responded into Mark's earpiece.

They waited in the woods, where plenty of places provided ample cover. Mark found a sturdy tree and climbed to a branch higher than the roofline of the building he'd just jumped off. Patience was crucial, but having the advantage of sight was even more important. He focused his sniper riflescope on the second-story roof. To his surprise, the reward for this decision came almost immediately. Two players simultaneously jumped to the single-story roof, but they weren't fighting each other.

They must be working together to survive . . . not a bad idea, but as the kill ratio gets close to the end, they'll eventually have to turn on each other . . . or maybe they're related. A family of killers . . . Mark had time to quickly think through all these ideas as he aimed.

As they ran toward Slowpry, he took two precise shots, only about a second apart. The bodies continued moving forward, although they had been hit from the front. They were moving so fast that they fell down face-first on the flat roofing material. It looked like a runner tripping badly at the Olympics. After hearing the noise of a successful pair of kills in their earpiece, Mark and Simon decided to leave. Those two bodies might alter the behavior of players coming later; they would not make the mistake of running toward the forest. It was an error that Mark and Simon survived by mere luck; Noah88 had followed a similar hiding tactic but had given up right before Slowpry showed up.

"We've been lucky so far," Mark cautioned Simon.

"I know. This is intense. We need a solid strategy to get to the water without being spotted," Simon whispered, thinking so hard that his head spun. "What would you do if you were in Vietnam or some other godforsaken place?"

"Try to blend in," Mark said. "We should disappear."

Slowpry jumped off the tree and began to run into the forest, hugging the edge of the prairie to maximize the mixture of speed and coverage. Running across an open field would prove foolish, no matter how much faster it allowed him to run. He searched for a clearing and turned into the forest sharply. He went to work pulling out weeds and branches from the trees. He checked in his online toolkit for twine. He tied the weed stalks all over his body, camouflaging as well as he could. His movements were precise as he cut different length branches for his arms, legs, and torso that would allow him to be invisible but still mobile. The avatar mimicked Mark's exact moves and the greenery quickly transformed Slowpry into an ugly bush navigating the forest's edge, safe from long-distance snipers. On the horizon, a tall hill looked like a perfect place to survey the surrounding area.

"We're moving to those hills," Mark informed him, not asking any longer.

"Okay. This is clever, by the way, this camo," Simon offered, genuinely impressed by how good it looked.

"Thanks."

Noah88 painstakingly reached his twenty kills by squatting in the root-system crevice of a huge tree and taking out players as they came down the path. He pulled them off the path after gunning them down and pushed the bodies off the hill and out of sight. It was a grueling and gory way to accomplish the task, but he chose the path of hard work and consistency. Yes, he risked being noticed and sniped from the forest, but that was a chance he had to take.

After clocking his twentieth kill, Noah88 headed for the lake he had spied from the top of the hill and drove the waiting boat toward the island in the distance, already celebrating in his mind. Once on land, he knew that he needed to reach the main plaza and avoid the guards to move forward. Noah88 stealthily crept toward the building in the distance, mindfully watching for any opponents.

The empty island was even more disturbing than the empty wasteland he had just left, so he opted to follow Rule Number Two: patience. He hid near the plaza entry and waited. A few hours later, another player arrived and entered the plaza. Noah88 positioned himself to view the outcome of this encounter. Slowpry moved into the center of the plaza, where three guards instantly charged at him, weapons swinging. Noah88 sprang into action after a split-second thought flashed into his mind.

Two players can beat three guards.

Slowpry was battling all three guards, and his energy meter was flashing in distress when Noah88 took down one guard from behind. The other two guards quickly fell as Noah88 pulled their attention away from Slowpry, who could finish them off.

"Thanks," Slowpry said.

"You're welcome," Noah88 replied, not knowing that Slowpry had tried to line him up in crosshairs about eight hours earlier.

"Shall we?"

Slowpry motioned for Noah88 to enter the central square of the floor pattern with him. They both stepped on it simultaneously and the victory ceremony began. It was a brand new and overwhelmingly elaborate celebration, but most of the details were forgotten by all three participants. The one thing they wanted was the individual invitation to the tournament, which they were eventually granted.

***

Noah's invitation meant taking his first trip outside the US. Dozens of instructions came with the invitation, but the timeliness of his departure was stressed above all else. Noah prepared over the next few days, gathering his passport, cash, his cell phone charger, a bag with clothing, and toiletries.

What Noah never prepared for was being a celebrity in New York. Thanks to Jane at Fast Messengers, his invitation to the Ultimatus tournament was leaked to the media. She mentioned Noah to a friend, who blogged about it, and invitations suddenly flooded Noah's inbox. One such offer was a "must go," at least from his perspective.

Two nights later, Noah was sitting in semi-shock in the green room of *The Colbert Report*. It was an entire suite where guests waited to go on the show; the live taping was being shown on a TV monitor hanging on the wall. Appetizers, junk food, soda, and booze all tempted Noah, but his nerves didn't allow him to touch anything. The main guest was sitting next to Noah, a famous astronomer named Lawrence Krauss. Noah had been invited to show up for a special segment for a few minutes at the beginning of the show.

"Mr. Jones?" A lovely female assistant snapped him from his reverie.

"Yes?"

"You're up. If you're all ready to go, you can follow me."

Noah walked down the white hallway lined with posters of Stephen Colbert receiving various awards or shaking hands with celebrities, politicians, and other recognizable figures. He stood, as directed, behind a short curtain from where he could see Stephen talking to his audience.

"Ladies and gentlemen," Stephen said to his audience. "As you know, I am a huge fan of these *video games* that you may have heard about. I've been playing Pong for years now and almost beat my nephew last Christmas, so . . . I clearly know what I'm talking about. My nephew is six." He paused for laughter; the screen showed Stephen playing Pong with a child on an antique TV set. "That's why I have invited my next, special guest, the winner of a championship that only a few video gamers have achieved . . . and he beat my nephew in Pong once!" Stephen laughed and pointed toward the opening in the set where Noah stood.

"Now!" Stephen's assistant pushed Noah out onto the stage. He stepped out into the lights and walked straight to Stephen's desk, where he shook Colbert's hand and struggled to keep his legs under him. Luckily, he was able to sit down almost immediately.

"Noah Jones, ladies and gentlemen, the receiver of an invitation to play in the final tournament of Ultimatus," Stephen introduced Noah to an applauding audience.

"Hi," Noah said, unsure of what the protocol was, having never been a celebrity or a guest on a national talk show before.

"Did I say that right? Ultimatus?"

"Ultimaytus. Ultimatuse, po-tay-to, po-tah-to. I'm not sure, frankly."

"Fair enough, but you're ready to win for America, right? We're number one in Ultimatus, isn't that correct?"

"Well . . . no, actually. This year, only two Americans received invitations. None of the actual champions have been American."

"What? Is this like soccer or something? Didn't we invent Ultimatus?" Stephen said in his iconic sarcastic tone. He frowned and looked down at his desk in mock sadness.

"I . . . don't think so," Noah answered and got a laugh from the audience, which bolstered his confidence.

"Fine. But tell us something, because we want to set the record straight. This game is evil, right? Like most video games?" Stephen asked in a faux-serious tone.

"You mean like Pong?" Noah replied. The audience loved Noah's second witty comment in a row. They laughed and clapped, even interrupting Stephen.

"Keep it down now; I'm trying to find out something here. You know what I mean, Noah, there are rumors out there . . . that Ultimatus is deadly. That players disappear?"

"I don't know about that. I certainly don't think so.

Maybe these rumors started because Ultimatus is hard for a lot of people. It's physically intense. You need to actually work, not just sit on a couch and punch buttons."

"What do you mean? You seem pretty fit, just like me. Why don't you show us some moves that you might need in the game?"

Noah removed his shirt and the women in the audience cheered and whistled. He moved like a martial artist and did a few lunges and jumps, mimicking what he might do to attack an opponent. Stephen was clearly impressed and continued with his non-stop comedy.

"Wow . . . the video game did all that to you? I'm going to have to kick Pong to the curb!" Stephen looked directly at the camera and addressed his nephew.

"Stevie, I can no longer play with you. You are a couch potato, and I hope that one day you get off that couch and learn how to play Ultimatus." Stephen turned back to Noah after delivering the joke. "Noah Jones, ladies and gentlemen—our first American Ultimatus champion!" Stephen shook Noah's hand, which was the sign that the interview was over.

Noah's feet barely touched the floor, as though he had a tether on the top of his head. He left the Nickelodeon building on a brilliant high, ready to continue the life of a fresh celebrity. He was pulled from his thoughts of international fame by the buzzing of a text in his pocket.

Be at JFK in two hours. Terminal 2. Iberia Airlines.

9

Stellan flew on a black-colored hang glider with a worker from the corporation who clearly knew what he was doing. In the pilot's helmet, Stellan could see an interior projection screen, which meant that the pilot could view some sort of navigation beacon. Stellan was glad to know that something was guiding them, because the dense fog allowed for less than ten feet of forward visibility. The beacon guided the pilot toward a destination anchored out in front of the Dover Cliffs: a large yacht owned by Ultimatus—*The Ultimus II*. The landing would be aquatic and could definitely be dangerous, but the operator didn't warn or instruct Stellan of anything; he simply went about his mission as if Stellan were little more than a crate of potatoes to deliver for dinner.

About a hundred feet from the yacht, which was now visible in front of them as the fog blew onward, the hang glider operator turned to Stellan, looked at him through the computer-lit helmet glass, and said one word.

"Goodbye."

He released the harness and Stellan fell into the ocean from fifty feet up. The hang glider continued forward and circled around the yacht. Other operators were on the exact same path, dropping their loads near Stellan. The other players were splashing into the water twenty or thirty yards from where Stellan was now treading water. The only option was to swim. All the players were fit, and any injuries sustained were minor. They all reach the huge boat's rear deck and climb aboard. The pilot splash landed gently on the ocean, very close to the yacht, and began swimming toward towlines that had been thrown out. They hooked their gliders to the lines and pulled them up via hoist tethers that the yacht had on its port-side door. Mega-yachts like *Ultimus II* included a toy storage area for their owner's to keep WaveRunners and other cool gadgets, like mini-submarines, for quick access to the ocean away from the engines. This grown-up playroom was the point of entry for the pilots. As soon as the last glider had been hoisted into the large port-side door, it slid shut and the yacht's motors spun into action.

Inside the *Ultimus II,* other company employees greeted the six players with decidedly better personalities than the hang glider operators. Stellan received a large towel to dry off with; he also drank the hot beverage that was handed to him. He was happy and relieved to have that stage of the voyage complete. Unsettled by the GPS episode, he began to put the pieces together, realizing that the only person that could have placed it there was Ingeborg. That fact made him uneasy—and angry. She had been very inquisitive about Ultimatus and he had revealed more than he probably should have. The loss of Ingeborg hurt him more than he had expected, but no one, not even her, was going to get in the way of his ultimate goal.

Other players were moving about in their towels and were being led to their cabins. None of them were speaking to one another. Stellan followed one of the staff members up the stairs to a spacious room, which must have been larger than most—the yacht was only so large.

Hierarchies in Ultimatus were respected, just as in any corporation, and Stellan had the upper hand—for now. His room was stunning in both its lavish decorations and its enormous size. The tournament the year before had been held at an island compound; it had been nothing like this. He decided that he liked his first taste of life in a mega-yacht. His stateroom had floor-to-ceiling windows and a sparkling bathroom made entirely of marble. It also had a shower large enough for four people, which Stellan used immediately. He found Reference-brand shampoo, just like the one that he regularly bought at his local store. In fact, all the bathroom's products were his preferred brands, a fact for which he was thankful, if slightly disturbed, as he had traveled empty-handed.

The experience for first-time tournament participants a floor below Stellan wasn't bad either. Their toiletries weren't personalized, but the Bulgari-brand products were quite nice. The rooms were smaller and the windows were round portholes, but the beds were luxurious, with seven-hundred-count sheets and soft down pillows. These players were finally living the dream they had been working toward for so long—they didn't care about having to use an unfamiliar type of shampoo.

By ten in the morning, the *Ultimus II* was heading full throttle toward *mare liberum*, approximately two-hundred nautical miles west into the Atlantic Ocean. It would take ten hours to reach their destination if they went in a straight line; they headed toward international waters as fast as the yacht could go. Players were summoned via intercom for lunch. This first meal revealed how many players were actually on the yacht and who they were. Stellan arrived early and was famished, not having eaten much the night before. The players all eyed one another and made short first-name introductions. A few players were talkative, but most were quiet—not wanting to converse with the enemy. Stellan's style leaned toward the latter; he did not intentionally seek anyone out for conversation.

"What's wrong, Mr. Firemist1?" Ricardo Rodriguez questioned him in a slight Mexican accent. "You don't want to meet any of the players?"

"I'm going to have to kill you. Why should I find a reason to like you?" Stellan answered. His grave tone and his strong, Swedish accent took the friendly wind out of Ricardo's sails.

"It's only a game. Relax, man," Ricardo said with knitted eyebrows and a small smile.

"Sure. Only a game. You can call me Stellan."

Stellan moved away from Ricardo and sat down at the head of the table, near the buffet. The staff wore completely black outfits with the Ultimatus logo on their shirt pockets. As soon as he sat, they began to serve Stellan as though he owned the yacht; they all seemed to know exactly who he was and where he sat in the game's hierarchy—basically he was royalty. Stellan didn't fully bask in this adoration as he had in the past. His ego was bruised, and that sort of psychological wound could be just as dangerous as a bullet to the head.

A few moments later, a gorgeous creature walked into the room. Stellan sprang up without even thinking, startling some of the new players sitting around the table. Gina walked in a rhythmic roll step straight to Stellan, standing unnecessarily close to him as they greeted one another.

"It's always a pleasure to see you, Gina," Stellan said, then kissed her on both cheeks in the Italian style.

Gina smiled and said nothing. Stellan pulled out a chair next to him, and she sat down.

"No hard feelings," Gina said.
"Of course not. We're both here, aren't we?"

Stellan had almost died in the previous tournament, and had luck not intervened on his behalf, Gina would have killed him. She took what would have been the fatal shot, and Stellan had resigned himself to death, but a tree branch in the program fell at the perfect moment, blocking his body an instant before the bullet struck him. He had never witnessed a random act of nature in the game actually save a player's life. It was a one in a billion chance, but he wasn't complaining. Her bullet would have killed him, but Stellan survived to play another day, meaning that one young and very talented player from the Czech Republic who would have made it to the top ten that year was bumped by Firemist1.

Did divine virtual intervention exist? Doubtful, but lucky programming certainly did . . . .

The meal consisted of delicious veal Milanese, a selection of steaming grilled vegetables, and a salad with a choice of a dozen dressings. No bread or sweets were offered. Also, none of the contestants were looking for desserts, soda, or any other quick calorie jolts. At this level, they knew what their bodies needed: full meals with complex carbohydrates. That was the only way to survive in the rarified air of an Ultimatus tournament. The quantity of vegetables and veal consumed by the group of twenty-four players was outrageous. The table became livelier as they ate; conversations were sparked left and right. The majority of the excitement flowed out of the new players; they had the most questions for the staff and also, if they were willing to start a conversation with veritable royalty, for the reigning tournament champs.

A disproportionate number of men to women was expected in gaming society, but the women here were young, intense, and cut like statues. In terms of their looks, some were stunning, like Gina, while others were somewhere on the other side of attractive. Sixteen men and eight women sat around the table; among them, there was not a pound of excess fat. It was like a dinner table at the Olympic Games Athlete Village.

"Is our host going to meet us?" most new players asked at one point or another.

"No, the CEO of Ultimatus will not be attending this lunch," the servers dutifully and repetitively answered.

"Fellini? So, do you call him by that name too?" Ricardo asked one worker near him.

"Yes. We are allowed to call him Fellini, and he is aware that this name is used in the outside world," a worker responded, as though every answer was scripted.

"So, what's his real name?" Ricardo continued; most of the table had quieted to hear the outcome of this exchange.

"We don't know," the Steve Jobs-attired worker answered.

"Come again?" Ricardo asked.

"We don't know. How many times have you asked for information about the person interviewing you for a job?"

Ricardo had nothing to say to that; it was a good point. He also didn't care that much; his mind was itching to play Ultimatus.

"This is the longest I've gone without playing," he said to no one in particular, quickly changing the subject.

"I know, me too. I'm dying to play," another new

player piped up.

"Don't worry. You'll get that wish soon enough," Gina cut in. The second player paused and swallowed, then forced a small laugh. Stellan chuckled and looked at her from the corner of his eye. He had forgotten how much fun Gina could bring to a room—she certainly kept things interesting. It was a real shame that he had dreamt of killing her so many times in the past year.

The *Ultimus II* was en route to a point due west of Cape Finisterre, off the coast of Spain. Once in international waters, the vessel would navigate under no country's political authority. This would be the final pick-up point for players. In Spain, Ultimatus had fewer issues, as its players were wiped clean at Santiago de Compostela. Security was considerably more relaxed than it had been in England. Even so, Fellini took no chances. The *Ultimus II* would be waiting in the high seas.

***

Finisterre was a popular destination for those of the Catholic faith. Most pilgrims that have been to worship at St. James Cathedral also made the walk to Cape Finisterre to end their pilgrimage in a symbolic arrival at the "End of the Earth." The number of such tourists varied from year to year, but it was always a steady stream, and the summers were usually crowded. This pilgrimage ritual was what Fellini counted on; the last six players were but a drop of humanity in this ocean of believers.

Mark received his instructions via text message, and he hurried to catch his flight from D.C. to Madrid. His coach ticket flew via a connection in NY with a large jumbo jet. When he exited the plane in Barajas International Airport, Mark went to the nearest bathroom and entered a stall, where he texted Simon with a second ghost phone. Simon had been up all night waiting to connect with Mark. He texted the contact name and location in Madrid for the drop-off. The CIA had tentacles everywhere in the world, but they couldn't control the TSA without making a big fuss; Simon did not want to risk a year of work by having Mark stand out for passing through TSA while acting suspiciously. The corporation might be following him all the way to the plane; he had no way of knowing for sure. A few minutes later, Mark received another text from the corporation with instructions to be on the next train to Santiago de Compostela. Mark had never been to Madrid, and he regretfully thought about missing the opportunity to visit any of the famous sights. He also couldn't simply call the agency's contact in Madrid. He needed to alert them, but couldn't risk being seen texting in the open. He proceeded to the train and texted from inside the cramped train bathroom.

If I'm being followed, then maybe they'll think that I have a stomach virus . . . Mark schemed an excuse in advance, so it would seem natural in case he was asked.

In Santiago, he had a reservation in a small hotel for two nights, but he didn't know how long the wait would be, so he had to work fast to meet the contact. He texted Simon the place to make the drop, as well as the time: the following morning at 9:10 a.m. The exchange would happen inside the Cathedral of Santiago at the Chapel of the Savior. The opening time for the cathedral, 9 a.m., appeared on the tourist guide in his room. The beautiful medieval structure had the typical cross plan, and Mark chose the chapel behind the main altar. He planned this in case he was being followed, as the altar would cover him from view for the few seconds of privacy he needed from whoever followed him to make the pick-up. Simon came up with "Is this the Savior?" as the code phrase to recognize the agent. It contained the name of the chapel, so saying it out loud would not raise any suspicions. The operation remained a go.

Simon had scrambled an operative to Santiago with equipment from the CIA headquarters in Madrid. The small package consisted of a few devices that looked like flash drives, a small earpiece, and a battery. The miniature device was capable of capturing wireless signals, but in their absence, emitted a GPS beacon. This high-tech equipment didn't send any signals when the battery was not attached, which meant that it couldn't be detected. Once assembled, it would have about a week of battery life with all of its functions, and up to a month or more of pinging the GPS. Mark's left shoe had a cavity already prepared in the inner sole to hide the entire package. The layers of rubber prevented moisture from penetrating the pocket. Mark would even able to swim, if needed, and the unit would still work once assembled.

Mark ate breakfast at 8 a.m. the following morning in the hotel's makeshift breakfast area. This was the lobby with additional tables brought in by the staff for that specific purpose. He ate three soft-boiled eggs and toast from the limited menu. At a quarter to nine, he walked from his hotel to the cathedral, surprised at how many people were doing the same. He didn't look back to scan for someone following him and kept a steady strolling pace. He subtly checked the time on his cell phone to control his pace and arrived exactly at nine.

As he moved through the narrow Avenida de Raxoli, he could not prepare himself for the emotions he was about to feel. The street suddenly turned right and he found himself standing at the southwest corner of an enormous plaza with four incredible buildings facing each other. To his right, the tallest building was the cathedral with its gigantic spires reaching higher than any building in Washington, D.C. Only the Washington Memorial might have been higher, but the cathedral was ancient. Its first level started after two huge staircases. Mark experienced something bigger than himself, as if the air had been sucked from his stomach. His love of traveling suddenly made him forget that he was at a critical point in the middle of a mission.

I can't believe this is here. The reality is a hell of a lot different than the photos.

He shook out of his daydreams and kept to the plan. It was easy to feign interest in the artistic glory of the cathedral, which gave a bit more time for the contact to reach the rear chapel. Mark waited, contemplating the work of masons who had toiled for centuries, before making his move. At 9:08, he entered the cavernous space and immediately quickened his pace to give him more time behind the altar. The cathedral was large enough to hold five thousand people, and as he walked toward the rear, the magnitude of the altar's richness made him pause.

The contact was a male field operative of about thirty, with red hair, who appeared more British than American. His entire outfit had been crafted to scream tourist. He even wore a camera around his neck, which looked ridiculous, considering that no one carried actual cameras anymore. The redheaded man stood alone at the Chapel of the Savior.

Mark entered the chapel and spoke softly; "Is this the Savior?"

Footsteps could be heard moving quickly through the cathedral. Without a word, the ginger CIA man placed a small cigarette pack-sized package in Mark's left jacket pocket and left. Mark walked to the chapel altar and kneeled without looking back. Someone entered the chapel a second later, sounding quite out of breath.

So I am being watched, Mark thought.

He elected to stay, pretending to pray for a few minutes. Mark eventually walked out of the chapel, leaving a single blonde woman in her late twenties, who was also pretending to pray. The drop had worked. Mark spent another hour in the church, reading and learning about Catholic traditions.

Kennedy was a Catholic. I wonder if he worshipped a bunch of old relics. If someone asks, I'll have to say that I'm a Catholic too. Or else that praying won't make much sense. He tried to remember if he knew any actual prayers from Catholicism.

Mark returned to the hotel and placed the equipment in his shoe's secret compartment, then burned the packaging in the bathroom. The material used by the CIA was made to burn with almost no smoke. Mark could have done this in the room, but extra care was warranted in such close quarters. The shoes sported heavy metal rings, metal shoelaces, and a steel toe. This was intentional, so the shoes would be purposefully noted by any metal detector, hopefully avoiding any further inspection.

Earlier attempts by various governmental agencies to infiltrate had failed primarily because the Ultimatus Corporation was impressively paranoid—to them, security was paramount. Fellini had to ensure that the tournament would be secure, especially when different law enforcement agencies from different countries came around to investigate. He crafted new and ever more elusive ways to counter their efforts and keep the location secure every year. The tournament was the biggest draw for new players; sales soared during these three days. The total number of viewers grew every year. The previous year's tournament had ten million computers logged in, which represented far more than ten million viewers, as their research said that gamer fans preferred to watch the tournament with groups of their friends.

With his communication device in place, Mark went back to sleep, exhausted from the jet lag. He walked around in the afternoon and hung out in the lobby lounge, keeping an eye out for any tourists that he thought might be players.

His CIA instructions were clear; he should only use the satellite communication device if and when he arrived at the tournament. The crowded hotel full of Catholic tourists was obviously not the location of the competition.

***

A year earlier, the CIA had failed to locate the tournament. The extensive planning that had gone into Mark and Simon's mission had stemmed from this fiasco. Director Stewart kept the events of last year sealed in top-secret files that even Senator George had been unable to access. Senator George's nephew, D. J., had been unaware of the GPS that the CIA had planted on his clothing.

In Marseille, the corporation had apparently found the GPS on the young man—he had been missing ever since. Robert felt partially responsible for D. J.'s disappearance, but perhaps more importantly, Robert needed to ensure that Senator George never found out that the agency might have been responsible for D. J.'s death. Robert had changed his strategy in this second year of the operation and decided to use actual field agents to penetrate the corporation in addition to the advanced GPS that could be enabled at the site once it was infiltrated. That sophisticated new tech was now lying dormant in the inner sole of Mark's steel-toed boots.

***

The waiting did not last long. That same evening, Mark received a text while he sat in the hotel lobby. One or two other guests stood up within a few minutes of one another, phones in hand. Judging from their slim physique, it was a safe bet that they were players. Mark would not get a chance to return to his room. The text was quite clear.

Walk out of the hotel immediately. There will be a procession of people. Follow it to Finisterre and do everything they do.

Mark left the hotel straight away, as instructed, and fell into the flow of pilgrims who seldom spoke, praying silently as they walked. He maneuvered near an oriental woman in her twenties whom he had spotted in the lobby.

"Do you speak English?" Mark asked.
"Yes, who doesn't?" Min Lin said suspiciously.
"In Spain, I didn't find too many."
"True, but for a Chinese person, English is necessary," Min replied, as though explaining something simple to an ignorant child.
"Are you a player?"

Min nodded. Both were clearly happy to have a companion operating under the same mysterious directions. Being shuttled around by text messages can unnerve anyone. They walked side by side, having said nothing except when they had exchanged names. Mark looked up to the sky, like many other pilgrims, although his heavenward gaze was not in prayer but in disbelief.

The procession continued to the end of the peninsula, nearly a mile away. At the end of the pilgrimage, a lighthouse stood, and a huge bonfire burned on the open terrace before it. Mark walked like the other pilgrims, but his military training helped him notice things that others might have missed. Pilgrims were walking back to the main town without shoes—every single one was barefoot!

Most pilgrims were wearing shoes on the way to the bonfire, but they were all taking their shoes off and throwing them into the fire once they reached the end of the peninsula.

What in the world is this ritual?

He had to think fast. As soon as he realized the predicament he was in, Mark dropped to the floor and pretended that something had happened to his shoe. Min stopped as he wrestled his left shoe off.

"I have a pebble in my shoe," Mark explained.

Amidst the darkness and confusion of pilgrims walking by them, Mark removed the entire inner sole of his left shoe and placed it slyly in his jacket pocket. He replaced the shoe and prayed that Min hadn't picked up on his deception. As soon as he finished this, he moved forward and tried his best to walk normally and prevent the height difference between his feet from being noticed. Min was clearly trying to figure out what the commotion ahead was all about. When they arrived at the bonfire, they did as expected and threw their shoes into the fire.

An instant later, they both received the following text:

Continue straight to the end of the land and down to the ocean front.

Min and Mark looked at one another and walked past the bonfire where hundreds of pilgrims knelt in prayer. Four or five more pilgrims also moved past the bonfire toward the ocean. A black-shirted corporation employee approached them with a bag in his hand. To any innocent bystander, it appeared as though he was collecting money for the church.

"Players?"
"Yes." Min and Mark answered in unison.
"Place your cellphones in here. Continue to that large rock," the anonymous employee instructed them in an emotionless tone and pointed at a large boulder behind him, near the shore.

This employee collected all six devices and left the peninsula, heading back to the hotel. He was the only one wearing shoes on the dark return road, but no one noticed.

In the darkness, shoeless, they were miserable. One player or another occasionally complained in a shouted outburst as the rocky path stabbed yet another foot. A flashlight ahead signaled them, and they were ordered to stop. In a small clearing, under a large rock formation, they could see the glistening blackness of the ocean roughly one hundred feet below. Barely noticeable in the dark night was a heavy-gauge wire attached to the huge boulder; its other end disappeared over the dark ocean at a steep angle. Each player was scanned with a wand by a sole corporation worker, who also operated the makeshift zip line.

"If you turn around, the water will hurt your face and genitals, so put yourself in this position," the operator of the impromptu zip line explained, demonstrating with his face angled toward the lighthouse, his legs raised as high as possible.

"You want to hit the water with your back and tailbone, followed by the rest of you. If you're still wearing shoes, take them off, or they will hurt your ankles when the water rips them off. If you have them, hand them to me. Nothing can stay behind at this location," he said, directing that last bit so that all six players could clearly hear.

Mark was relieved that the burning ceremony had been planned by Fellini, not because of his specially altered shoes, but because of their mode of transportation. The religious ceremony had simply helped to avoid any evidence of the shoes being left behind. Fellini had planned the tournament on a new moon to guarantee the darkest possible conditions. Mark used the same pitch-black night to his advantage, quickly hiding the inner sole in a crevice among the rocky hills. The device within the rubber sole wasn't supposed to be detectable by a wand device but he didn't want to take any chances. Getting the GPS all the way to the tournament location was priority number one.

I'll get scanned and then grab it before I zip out, Mark planned.

The operator took the first player by his hand, put his grip on the T-shaped handle of the pulley system, and checked that he was holding onto it firmly. The player had no time to think, and given how hell-bent he was likely to be in the tournament, he wasn't about to start complaining.

"Hold on hard and don't let go until you're fully stopped. Then, swim away. Understood?" the operator asked gruffly.

"I think so . . . " answered the player uncertainly.

"Off you go," the operator passively stated. With that, the player stepped to the edge of the cliff.

"But where am I going?"

"To the plane."

Mark overheard that the zip line ended at a plane down in the dark ocean. *A bold move. How could anyone follow them once the line was removed?*

The Ultimatus worker waved his flashlight toward the sea in a series of bursts and halting gestures. From the middle of the dark ocean, the players could see bursting patterns of light in response. The noise from the first player descending whirred into the sky. They could faintly hear the sound of the plane engine below. About a minute later, the operator grabbed another pulley with a T-shaped handle and attached it to the cable.

Min was next, and she looked determined— excited almost. She looked at Mark and made a face that silently said, "Here goes nothing." Mark helped Min up onto the rock and stood by her, as if he were her boyfriend or something. The operator expected only one, but used the wand on both players; once Mark was swept, he stepped back. He recovered the inner sole with a few more backward steps and deftly placed it in his crotch as Min grasped her T-handle.

Min looked a bit more nervous now that she stood at the edge; she was peering over, as if trying to determine if the player before her had survived the one-way trip. The worker sent flashlight bursts again, and when the bursts from below flashed back, the five players, and even the operator, were relieved. These bursts seemed to soothe Min, and she was sent off into the darkness. Mark immediately approached the operator. He needed the operator to see that it was him and that he had already been swept.

Luck sided with Mark; he was given a new pulley, which Mark helped to clip on the wire. Without waiting for direction, Mark placed himself in position and looked back at the ocean, waiting for the light bursts to follow Min's descent. The operator had deviated so slightly from his orders, he didn't give it a second thought. He was supposed to sweep and send every player one at a time. Leaving Mark swept and unguarded for those extra seconds had been enough.

Mark zipped down like a rocket. If his feet hadn't been held up, he would have likely hit rocks. Keeping his abdominal muscles in a full crunch was absolutely necessary. The water hit his butt as if he had broken through a sheetrock wall. Winded and in pain, he relaxed when he felt the inner sole securely in his shorts.

Within the next five minutes, all the players and the operator were inside a Grumman HU-16 Albatross that had been rented by the corporation. They were battered and wet but alive and well. The second Ultimatus Corporation operator that had been signaling with his flashlight greeted them with towels and a smile.

This type of Grumman seaplane was the favorite of coast guards around the world, but many had also fallen into private hands. The seaplane was a versatile bird and could land almost anywhere. The engines had been running throughout the operation, and the pilot's orders instructed him to keep the steel line at a specific angle, always touching or nearly touching the water. This way, the arriving players would be stopped by the water without any risk of crashing into the plane. With all the players on board, the pilot moved away from the coast. The zip line stretched until it was torn from the hill by the powerful twin engines. The remaining cable whirred into a reel on the Albatross's side door. Once the end of the cable reached the door, the plane began to accelerate.

The takeoff was a long and bumpy ride; all the

players sighed when the airplane finally took to the air. They headed straight out to sea into a pitch-black sky. The late summer night was so dark that the gamers were almost immediately disoriented. Mark knew the Grumman HU-16, and its range, quite well. He calculated how only after three or four hours they would be past the point of no return, so he instead concerned himself with drying his body. He was still in a decent amount of pain from hitting the water at such a high speed. Fellini wanted to make sure that these arrivals were all real players; the physical conditions of the stunt had required them to be.

They were all told to sit down for the descent only an hour into the flight. The Albatross landed on the Atlantic Ocean approximately two-hundred-and-thirty nautical miles from the coast and was met by a large vessel at a previously appointed GPS rendezvous point. Mark looked out the small window, and a huge yacht stared back at him. A wave of relief swept over him; he gestured to Min to approach the window. Min's mouth opened and a smile formed.

"You have a lovely smile," Mark said without thinking
"Thank you," Min replied, her blush obvious even in the darkness.

A small dingy approached the Grumman. The six players and two operators got in, which made the plastic inflatable boat somewhat cramped. These nine figures drove in silence back to the *Ultimus II* and entered through an open side door. The Grumman turned around and began the lengthy run along the water for its second bumpy takeoff before it returned to Vigo, Spain.

10

In the waiting room of Director Stewart's office,
Simon paced nervously, making the director's secretary
uncomfortable.

"Please sit down," she admonished.
"I'm sorry, Mrs. Ratner," Simon said sheepishly and
sat down.
"He should be here soon. Would you like something
to drink?"
"Do you have any coffee?" he asked.
"Are you serious, Simon? You look like a nervous
wreck!"
"Oh, right. Of course. No. Yeah, that's okay.
Thanks." She was right. He could barely put a sentence
together.

Simon grabbed the previous day's condensed *WSJ*. The leaflet had only the most important world news in a summarized format prepared for high-level government officials. That day's leaflet would be on the director's desk. On the cover, it showed wars, famine, health crises, and dramatic economic news. The Ultimatus gaming problem would not make these pages—ever. Although the world might never know, Simon still had a CIA life-or-death crisis on his hands.

Robert Stewart entered his office vestibule and nodded to Mrs. Ratner, who summoned Simon from the waiting room with a similar nod.

"Just came back from a boring luncheon. What seems to be the problem?" Robert asked.

"No contact with Mark for over thirty-six hours, sir," Simon spat out anxiously.

"This is a problem because . . . ?"

"Well, Fellini is clearly an expert at detecting devices. If that GPS communication device on Mark was found, then he's been exposed. He could already be dead." Simon had clearly jumped to worst-case-scenario thinking.

"We don't know that yet," Robert said calmly. "Our report says that he departed the peninsula of Finisterre, Spain on a zip line and reached a sea plane, which flew toward the mid-Atlantic. The seaplane returned to Spain with no passengers; the pilot was interviewed by Spanish Interpol. Mark is on a yacht somewhere in international waters."

"You've read the report," Simon said, unable to hide his surprise. Robert ignored the question.

"And there's not much we can do right now. So why take up my time with this?" Robert asked cruelly.

"Well, sir, if he was caught, then he could be dead," Simon repeated.

"He could also be waiting for the right moment to turn on the GPS, or he could have burned the device with his shoes," Robert replied rationally.

"But that's crazy! Mark had orders to abort if he lost the device."

"Initiative, Simon. Some soldiers thrive by its virtues . . . some don't. We chose him because he wouldn't abort a mission because of some technicality."

"Wait, so you are okay with him going without a return ticket?" Simon was visibly agitated and began pacing around the vast office.

"Simon, relax! You seem extremely anxious over this. I know that you're still figuring out how things work around here. I want you to keep scanning for the device. Mark will need you to help him win the stupid game. For all we know, losing the tournament is the actual danger. Now go."

Simon left the office feeling as bad as when he had arrived, if not worse. Director Stewart showed a shockingly low level of concern for Mark's life but was completely abreast of the operation. Simon returned to his office and found his assistant, as bored as ever, looking for a signal on an otherwise blank screen.

***

On board the *Ultimus II,* the thirty finalists were having lunch on the main outside deck. The teak floors and the pristinely white surfaces of the yacht, together with the handsome group of players in their youthful prime, combined like an Abercrombie & Fitch ad campaign. The rest and relaxation were healthy rewards for the hours of gaming they had all invested to get there. Mark had no idea that his own Slowpry avatar had worked his way to a tournament invite faster than anyone in the history of Ultimatus—nor did any of the other players. Only Fellini had access to those types of details.

"You what? You had to hang glide in the middle of the night? And we were already on board?" Ricardo Rodriguez questioned, obviously surprised.

"I didn't say the middle of the night. It was very early morning. You where probably still asleep when we were dropped off the gliders into the ocean after flying off the White Cliffs of Dover!

"I woke up at nine." Ricardo bragged.

"How did you get here?" Stellan said and sipped his margarita.

"We were invited to a party on the *Ultimus II* at an Ibiza yacht club. We just stayed after the party ended," Ricardo boasted. "It was a hell of a good party, too!"

"You were lucky then; we were zip lined from a cliff to a sea plane . . . very painful," Min explained.

She sat opposite Stellan and Ricardo at a table; Mark sat by her side.

"I would have loved to have flown in or zip lined!" Ricardo said, like a child upset to have missed out on ice cream.

"Well, I would have loved to party my way in," Mark shot back as he stood up and raised his T-shirt to show them what appeared to be a black and blue island on his back. Some cringed at the mark on his body but they all laughed, perhaps forgetting for a moment that they would all be trying to kill one another soon.

The *Ultimus II* drove toward the sunset into the Atlantic Ocean. Looming in front of them was a small, semi-abandoned island, a distant piece of the Azores archipelago. Fellini had prepared this island for the 5th Ultimatus Tournament. A few years back, Fellini's Ultimatus didn't exist, yet he had quickly become the most powerful game owner in the world. The most impressive achievement was not in rising so quickly to the top, which had often happened to many gaming companies in the past, but rather in structuring his game to evolve and stay in the top spot for five years in a row.

Companies rose to the top, but quickly found that teens tired of their games and dropped them just as fast as they adopted them. Ultimatus constantly challenged players physically and intellectually, but the day Fellini devised the tournament and added monetary rewards for players was the real turning point. This year, the tournament would be held in a makeshift construction that had been prepared throughout the past year. Creating the thirty cubicles required for gaming and installing temporary wiring to them had been easy. Fellini's new tournament location ended up looking like a Philippine slum. The ceiling was made of corrugated metal, and the walls were simple wooden panels.

The real work was in creating the tournament's map and ambiance within the game. The players didn't care that the floor was a concrete slab or that the nearest bathroom was a makeshift outhouse separated from the gaming pods . . . they were living in the game.

All the players knew that the tournament would start the following day, so they all had some fun but were also carefully controlling their liquor and sugar intake. These thirty premier athletes were directed to the living room as night fell. A company employee turned on a large flat screen and waited for it to warm up before pressing play.

A short movie about Ultimatus came on, telling the story from its first design to the present version. It consisted of highlight reel kill scenes, victory ceremonies, and even famous players' avatars, such as Gina's BlingBlingBaby and Stellan's Firemist1. Then, the screen went black. White letters unfurled on the screen:

"A message from the founder—Fellini."

Fellini's avatar appeared on the screen. His facial expressions were moving, which was not the norm in the game. The avatar was white, blue-eyed, and slightly blonde. In the distance, a lush, green valley sat before large mountains, behind which a pinkish-hued sky and two moons hung. Fellini's avatar was like a better-looking version of Rob Lowe, similarly showing no aging.

"Welcome to the *Ultimus II*. Its crew and I want to wish you a happy stay. You are about to begin the 5th Annual Ultimatus Tournament, a challenging and exhilarating experience. Many of you have worked for years to reach this point. As you know, the tournament is a battle to the death. When your avatar dies, as explained to you in the contracts that you have all accepted, you will cease to exist as well. You will never get to play Ultimatus again. We make sure of this."

A number of younger players turned to one another with instant concern. They had never read the terms and conditions; who does?

"You need to understand that being a paid player is a privilege that you have won with your skill. The mere fact that you are here means that you are at the top of your game—you've made it to historical heights. Luck, skill, strength, and knowledge . . . all of these attributes define you. You have now arrived at your goal. Your fame will continue to grow. If you reach the top ten, you will have a guaranteed annual income of one million euros."

Ricardo glanced at Stellan with an envious look and an admiring smile. Stellan just shrugged his shoulders in response.

"Who wants to play a game forever anyways? Who

even can?" Fellini continued with a lighter air to his speech. "You need to understand that this tournament is a serious endeavor. Here at Ultimatus, we monitor every decision and move you make in order to keep making this the most successful game in history. We are making history in more ways than one. Therefore, for this tournament, we will be revealing various special moments that will both challenge and entertain you. I won't be giving you a map of where the tournament will take place; I need you to discover these new worlds on your own. However, you should know that they are some of the best virtual maps that we've ever created. I hope you enjoy them. Rest up tonight. At 10 a.m. tomorrow, the 5th Annual Ultimatus Tournament begins."

The screen went black and all the players clapped at their hero, Fellini.

They broke ranks and went off to their private quarters. The *Ultimus II* had room for a crew of fifty and a passenger capacity of far more than these thirty players, all in full luxurious accommodations. The elevator and stairs led one flight down to the best rooms and a further floor down to the still-stunning mid-level rooms.

The highest deck housed the master bedroom suite. The crew lived on the third level down in rooms with porthole windows that occasionally dipped below the water line. The *Ultimus II* cruised at its highest speed of twenty-eight knots thanks to the booster engines that Fellini had recently refurbished. This 266-foot yacht was not the largest in the world, nor the fanciest, but it was worth well over the $150 million that Fellini had paid for it during the last financial crisis. Fellini had commissioned major overhauls in the yacht's interior design, improved the engine's functionality, and made massive technology updates.

The ship arrived at the north face of a nearly deserted island and maneuvered at five knots to back into the shantytown pier city where the tournament would happen. Once parked, the vessel quickly began to disappear from view. Workers began to move beams and corrugated metal roofing materials, as well as old wooden pallets and walls to cover the top of the yacht and the main exit hatches.

Large concrete beams were slid over the yacht on prepared rollers positioned at various spots on the top level of the yacht. The structure then hooked to these beams, making the yacht a part of the structural integrity of the town. In the hours the night provided, the entire shantytown structure covered the pier as well as the huge yacht. This was like a supermodel wearing an overcoat that belonged to a city bum. From the inner rooms of the boat, the players were unable to see anything outside but darkness. The main door hooked to a short bridge leading to the inner hallway, which circled around the boat, allowing entry to each gaming cubicle.

Each cubicle was equipped with the exact same equipment. It didn't matter which player entered which cubicle, considering that they wore the same equipment and logged into their accounts when they entered the tournament. On Saturday morning, the 5th Annual Tournament would begin, and over ten million men, women, and children from around the world would be watching these thirty champions compete from the middle of the Atlantic Ocean.

Live.

***

Mark awoke at 0600 hours GMT, well in advance of 0800, which was the time enforced by the corporation.

The tournament began at 1700 GMT, which was twelve
noon in Washington, D.C. He needed to test the
equipment and verify its viability after its arrival on the
Ultimus II. He opened a drawer in the cabin, pulling it all
the way out and turning it upside down. The shoe sole
glued to the back of the drawer was still there. The sole
had self-sticking glue behind a peel-off label, courtesy of
the CIA design team. Mark pried off the top layer of
sealed plastic.

The equipment looked fine. He removed the back
of the minute earpiece, and from a larger container, he
took out the plastic battery case with the only metal
component hidden in its center. This battery was a tiny
piece of metal, about the size of a lentil bean, packed
inside a cocoon-like case about fifteen times its size. The
cocoon covered the small battery, making the device
invisible even to modern X-ray machines, while the
specially designed plastic layers prevented the detection of
any metal. Once installed, the battery powered the
earpiece in his ear. The outer layer of the instrument had
been prepared with ear- hair implants that perfectly
matched Mark's hair type. It was a masterpiece of
miniature stealth technology. The earpiece connected to
another, slightly larger device, about the size of two
stacked quarters, via Bluetooth technology. The larger
battery for the Bluetooth device also came in a cocoon
similar to the earpiece battery's. Once the batteries were
installed, the two pieces of equipment would pair
automatically.

About 2,200 miles from the *Ultimus II,* a small ping
registered in a computer terminal at Langley, VA. Simon
was sleeping in front of the monitor, and it took a few
dozen pinging sounds for him to realize that he was finally
hearing the sound he'd been waiting for. He jumped up
and entered the pairing code, which would enable the
system to communicate via satellite with Mark. The signal

from the tiny device was coming from the middle of the Atlantic Ocean. He put on his headset and began to speak.

"Mark, Mark, come in Mark," Simon said.

"Hello. Can you hear me?" Mark's voice whispered back.

"Yes, just barely. Are you okay? I'm so glad that you're—"

"I'm speaking quietly. It's early, and I don't want to get caught," Mark spoke softly as he entered the bathroom and flushed the toilet.

"Mark, please keep the unit on. We're getting your coordinates now," Simon replied.

"Good. I can't speak much. Maybe during the game . . . if I need you."

"I'll be here. Have a good night."

"Are you kidding? We're being prepped this morning for the tournament," Mark explained, glad that his CIA counterpart was as ready as he was for the mission.

"Sorry, sorry . . . I just got the details on the time zone. Don't worry; I'll be ready for the tournament," Simon finished.

"Over and out."

Mark clicked off the larger device to save the Bluetooth battery; the GPS would continue relaying the beacon to the CIA. Meanwhile, Simon called Mrs. Ratner to give her and Director Stewart the good news.

Mark began his daily routine, which started with physical training. He did single sets of cardio and yoga maneuvers to warm up his body for what lay ahead. Oddly enough, he was more relaxed than the night before, even with the tournament only a few hours away, because he now knew that a rescue operation was at least a possibility.

However, somewhere in his gaming mind, he was

more relieved that now he could concentrate on winning this damn tournament.

***

Only a hundred feet away, Stellan was also awake and going through his morning exercise routine, just like Mark. He was flexing in a larger room with a queen-sized bed in which Gina continued to sleep. Gina and Stellan had a past that could fill a tabloid page or two, but the corporation forbade relationships on a more permanent level, so they knew that their history should stay on a purely physical level. They had agreed not to share anything about these trysts with anyone.

Regardless of their physical attraction to one another, they both knew that they would constantly meet online as adversaries and that they might have to eliminate one another. This latest meeting had not resulted in the steamy sex of past tournaments. Stellan simply held Gina tightly as they fell asleep; she understood from his emotional state that she was dealing with a wounded animal. Stellan had fallen for Ingeborg, and it had clearly been a hard fall. In love, the heart rules, not the brain. In other words, Stellan had already forgiven her for planting the GPS in his belt. He couldn't deny that he missed her and had already made up his mind to return to Stockholm and try to make it work with her. He knew that this was not the time for his mind to be distracted, but the heart can also be a terrible master.

This spectacular cabin facing the open waters of the Atlantic, complete with the two young people in their prime, had been wasted to a certain degree. Stellan's confidence and motives had shifted; Gina understood this. She also knew that those types of mental shifts could be more lethal in the game than any weapon loss or flawed strategy. Ultimatus was a game of confidence; Stellan's mindset was not conducive to success. That being said, he was still one of the best players of all time, if not the best, after Fellini himself, and his fame was enormous. When kids were lucky enough to encounter Firemist1, they would get an unforgettable rush. It meant certain death, obviously, but meeting the famous legend of Firemist1 seemed like a worthy trade-off. Sometimes, other players would ask him questions, and he occasionally took the time to give them a few priceless pointers. However, people mostly wanted to ask him what it was like to make a living by playing. Stellan would always answer with the same stock reply: "I live to play, and now I can live through playing—nothing is better."

Stellan finished warming up for the beginning of the tournament and went to the window to open the shades—pitch-black. He opened the window and stuck his head outside the yacht. His eyes adjusted and the concrete structure three or four feet in front of him came into view. The ship was eerily still, as if in a massive, yacht-sized car park. Looking up, he could see metal roofing material, but no sky. *What the hell?* One level below, Mark opened his own small, round window and discovered the strange concrete wall. He pushed his head out the window to check that they were still on water.

Not a dry dock, Mark mused in silence, momentarily unaware that he was being watched from above.

Well, at least the American is awake, Stellan thought to himself.

Mark unexpectedly glanced up and met Stellan's eyes staring down at him. He saw the metal roof above at the same time, frowned slightly, and then nodded to Stellan, sharing a rather cold, "hello." They both pulled their heads back inside and returned to their exercise routines, focusing on the things they *could* control.

***

The tournament was set to start at noon. Fellini always chose the summer months for the event, but had always kept the exact date a secret. Simon had no prior knowledge, except from the official Ultimatus corporation publicity that the Internet had to offer. The existence of the game and its followers was only known widely to gamers via the Internet; it was rarely a part of normal society. TV broadcasts and news channels carried little to no information about Ultimatus. There was only the occasional comment on certain financial networks regarding the staggering profits of the gaming industry, particularly its leading company. The online information on Ultimatus's website showed that the tournament would start in a world with rural and uninhabited conditions; the avatars in the short clip were exposed to vast valleys and soaring mountain peaks. This landscape was right out of the tundra in New Zealand or Tierra del Fuego on the tip of Argentina.

Miles away from America, Mark was nervous that Simon's input would be useless due to the huge distance and the different set-up; *what if there was a delay?* On the other hand, Simon was confident that the tactical advantage of being in Mark's head would work. In this tournament, Mark would benefit from Simon's input, considering that he had access to the live game and the location of every player on the map. Simon would be a remote bird's-eye view for Mark's avatar.

Mark will survive, Simon told himself for the hundredth time. *I wonder how the players are killed. There haven't been any traces of dead players, so how can we tell if it's the equipment or a simple shot to the head? Maybe they're not even dead . . . .*

Unfortunately for Simon, every possibility was still wide open—yet another unknown variable. He called Director Stewart to ask for the placement of a ship near the ping site; he received a quick snapback message.

"We have the full cooperation of the Portuguese authorities on this."

Simon looked in his CIA manual for the contact in the Portuguese Division and made the call. After speaking with the police station operator in Punta Delgada, Azores, Simon was put through to the agency consulate in Portugal.

"Hello, Mr. Diaz. This is Simon Prince from Headquarters in Langley," Simon said.

"Yes, Mr. Prince. What can I do for you?" Mr. Diaz replied in a strong Portuguese accent. He was thirty-seven years old, a weathered police detective in a small and truly boring town. With black hair, brown eyes, fair skin, and the beer belly of a much older man, he fit in quite well in Portugal. By averaging all Portuguese men, you would come close to something like Mr. Pedro Diaz.

"There is a small island on the Azores archipelago, and I need to send a team to investigate," Simon hastily explained.

"The name of the island?" Mr. Diaz asked; he seemed like an oddly direct man.

"The coordinates are 39.714777, -31.108989. I think it's called Corvo?"

"Corvo is small and empty, but I'll check and see what I can do. How soon do you need to have this look-see?"

"ASAP. My operative might be in grave danger," Simon continued.

"But Corvo is a protected island; there's virtually no development on it. Are you sure, Mr. Prince?"

"Yes. We need to send a ship immediately. Or even

better, a surveillance plane."

"Alright. Let me work out what we can do. I will get back to you tomorrow." Mr. Diaz was calm; his pleasant voice was like a travel agent with years of experience controlling tourists in panic mode.

"Mr. Diaz, we need this today!"

"I am afraid that today will be impossible. I am not a magician, Mr. Prince."

Mr. Diaz sounded even calmer than before, which irritated Simon even further.

"I will call you back."

"Mr. Diaz?"

Simon was speaking to the tone of a hung-up phone.

Becoming ever more sleep-deprived, Simon realized that he needed to manage his time better, or he would be useless to Mark. He moved under his desk, where he had a heavy coat lying on the floor. He slept with his phone alarm set to wake him at 11:00 a.m. EST. This allowed time for cleaning up and eating something before the actual tournament began. On other desks, CIA experts watched their screens and performed their menial or crucial jobs, completely oblivious to Simon and Mark's predicaments, and vice-versa.

Simon felt oddly alone, but as he had partially expected from this job, long and lonely streaks were the rule, not the exception.

11

The tournament players ate a hearty lunch from a buffet that had been set up in the dining room. The difference this time was that, although it was daytime, the room was lit by the ceiling's electric LED lights as if it were the middle of the night. Outside the windows, the view of the concrete walls depressed the spirit, but the players didn't care—their minds were focused on a different world. Mark detected a change in Gina's countenance; her body language revealed that something had changed. He made his move and sat down next to her.

"Hi, BlingBling," Mark opened confidently.
"Good day," she replied cordially in her seductive Italian accent, looking at Mark as if seeing him for the first time. Her attitude opened up slightly; she realized that he was more handsome from close up.
"You seem different somehow."

"From what? You don't know me."

"From the ruthless killer that you are."

"Ha. Ha. Ha." She left a slight pause between each *Ha,* accenting how false it was.

"Okay . . . okay. So, I'm not very good at small talk. So shoot me."

"I will."

Mark moved closer to her and whispered. He took a chance, but he needed to test his theory.

"You know that players die when they're killed in the game, right?"

"It's in our contract," she answered coolly.

"You read the terms and conditions?"

"Of course. Didn't you?"

"Nobody reads the terms and conditions."

Gina emitted a real laugh this time, and her smile was actually a delight.

"No, I'm serious. I didn't read them. Do they actually say that you can get killed?" Mark said, pretending to be ignorant. The electronic contract was written in much the same manner that airline ticket contracts are.

"They actually do," Gina replied seriously.

"So, if you kill me in the game, then BANG—I'm just dead?" Mark dropped his head on his plate with his tongue out, feeling slightly silly beside this beautiful maniac.

She laughed again. "I don't want that to happen to you."

"Then don't kill me."

"So are you sitting here trying to make me like you so that I'll have some compassion for you in the game?" Her tone had changed slightly.

"Nailed it!" Mark smiled and kept his eyes locked straight on hers. She felt something for this Mark character. He was a bit dumb, but he seemed sincere, and he was built like Adonis. She shook her head; thinking about anyone as something besides a potential target was a mistake.

"Don't count on finding any mercy out there." She stared straight into his eyes, but he didn't flinch like most men did around her. She liked that.

Their shared moment was interrupted by another announcement. The face of Fellini's avatar welcomed them on a large TV screen. The difference this time was that his avatar paused and talked as if it was an actual live conversation. Fellini spoke directly into a microphone from his office, which was twenty-five feet above them. There were no cutaways to pre-recorded introductions or video montages. Silence filled the room as he spoke.

"My friends, players, champions, you are thirty strong and will begin the 5th Annual Tournament in two hour's time. This year, we will have three maps, as in the past, and the rules are the same. The first map will last until ten kills are recorded. The remaining twenty players will have a rest period of eight hours. The second map will last until five more kills are recorded. Then there will be a rest period of four hours. The last map will begin with fifteen players and will end once five are killed. The remaining ten will be awarded the highest level of the game, unless they are returning champions, that is. Then, we will celebrate their victories as they deserve," Fellini said, and then added emphatically, "May the best ten remain on to play for Ultimatus!"

The screen went black, and a corporation employee opened a door to a makeshift canvas corridor that led up six steps to a short bridge, which was connected to the concrete structure. All the players exited in single file and were guarded by Fellini's handlers. The pathway led to a long oval-shaped corridor with a concrete wall facing the ship and wooden walls on the opposite end, as well as makeshift doors. Noah recognized the cheap hinges of the doors as being similar to the gate hardware of the dog run in his parents' house in San Diego. This whole rough and rugged set-up seemed strangely at odds with the luxury of the yacht.

The players were told to enter any of the thirty doors and settle in. No rooms were assigned, as all of them contained identical equipment. Once they were in the rooms, Fellini's assistants wrote the avatar names of the players in the various rooms on the doors in large letters, making them their own.

The players were all itching to head into these awful accommodations, not because they were bored by the decadence of the yacht, but because they were all essentially in withdrawal from not gaming for the past three or four days. To many of them, this was an intolerable amount of time, and they practically ran into the rooms for a real hit of their virtual drug.

Concrete walls divided the rooms on one side, but the other three walls were made of wood panels that looked weathered and old. On the far wall, the large windows to the outside had no shutters or glass; you could walk out of these to a cantilevered terrace that jutted about ten feet farther than the room, but there was no railing. The roof was made of corrugated metal and provided no heat insulation inside. Some players opted to keep the doors open in their rooms to provide draft ventilation. Those that did this were clearly smarter, or had experience in previous tournaments; every player vented their rooms eventually.

Inside each room were three large flat-panel displays mounted on the concrete wall. There was a center panel with two projecting arms holding the right and left screens at forty-five-degree angles. A small table with toy guns and clips, as well as a sniper rifle and a knife, was lying nearby. These gaming parts were Ultimatus equipment that was already familiar to the players. Of course, each room also had a one-size-fits-all Ultisuit for each player. Some rooms had mountainous terrain outside their windows, while others had direct ocean views, but the oval shape of the terraces jutting out of the rooms allowed all the players, once they stood on the terrace, to see where they were. From a distance, the entire structure resembled a small shantytown erected on a pier. From afar, this did not look like a destination of any kind; rusty roofs, decrepit wood-panel walls, no windows . . . it was abandoned and empty. Fellini had designed this structure to hide the yacht and had managed to build it with inexpensive material brought in on local fishing vessels. The concrete structure had been poured quickly from a large ship made to pump tons of ready-mixed concrete in a single day.

As soon as the players entered their respective rooms, they immediately went for their equipment, like drunks to the bottle. Stellan was the first to don the Ultisuit, and he shot the image of his own avatar on the main computer screen, which displayed all thirty players in a row. The avatars were similarly dressed in dark colors; they were only distinguishable by gender as their body types and hair color changed. Each avatar had a name floating over its body, which made the identity specific. Stellan shot at "Firemist1" and he instantly moved to a secondary screen where he entered his unique password. He turned left and right to check whether anyone was in the room before doing this. He didn't realize that there was a small camera looking at him from behind that sent his image to a central control room aboard the *Ultimus II*. Fellini sat watching more than fifty screens in a round room. He was a forty-five-year-old white male with unremarkable features. He was unmemorable—a ghost.

All the players did the same as Stellan and logged in

to reach the commencement ceremony. Mark had the earpiece in place and had turned on the Bluetooth device hidden in his underwear as they walked to their rooms. As he had expected, the room had a small closed-circuit camera pointed at him from behind. The screen obviously had an adapted camera as well. They could observe and record his every move. He would need to disable the cameras looking at him if he was going to have any freedom of movement.

Mark wore his Ultisuit, but before activating his avatar, he opened the door for ventilation and moved toward the windows. He stepped outside to the concrete slab terrace, sans railing. All around him were cliffs and ocean; he tried to plan ahead, but did not even know where this godforsaken place was.

In a nearby game room of identical proportions and details, Noah was finishing installing his suit. The commencement ceremony began, and his heart pounded audibly in his own ears. He had arrived. Now, finally, everyone he cared about would be able to watch him play and understand what he'd been working toward for so long. He would show them all.

***

In the San Diego living room of Noah's parents' home, the family sat in bated silence. Noah's brother turned on their web-enabled TV to www.ultimatus.com and prepared to experience the live tournament. Noah had traveled abroad; they knew this because he had asked for his birth certificate in order to get a passport. His mom had mailed the certificate along with a wallet-sized picture of the family. He had that memento on him as he strapped into the Ultisuit. His parents lived in the Kensington area in a detached three-bedroom, two-bath home in a Spanish style—they were typical middle-class stock. His father was a master builder and his mom was a yoga instructor; the last career they had imagined for their Noah was this crazy lifestyle of paid gaming. They still hoped that this was a passing phase, but they really didn't know what to expect. They saw the avatar name "Noah88" hanging over a dark figure on the screen. Not all parents shared in their children's gaming careers; as a matter of fact, Noah's parents were the exception. Most parents outright ignored their children's gaming obsessions altogether.

"It's so unlike Noah to be so dark and drab," Noah's mother said—a banal statement that only a mother could make.

"Survival, dear. He can't stand out too much. See? Look at all the other players," her husband explained, as though he were an expert on the entire subject, as only fathers can pretend to be.

***

The commencement ceremony took place in a downtown setting similar to Mexico City's famous square plaza, El Zocalo. The buildings were computer copies of this style, and from a large window in what would be the main government building, a figure stood looking at thirty avatars on the plaza—Fellini.

"Good day to all the players in the tournament and to all those players watching from the comfort of their homes," Fellini began. "I want to inaugurate the 5th Ultimatus Tournament and congratulate all of you on earning an invitation; merely being here is already a victory. Let the game begin!"

Fireworks exploded from behind the palace and daylight changed to night in a few short seconds. In the sky, where the fireworks burst, a white light made by the huge firework explosions created a sort of screen, where projections began to play snippet clips of past tournament moves and players reaching different levels. A player achieved Bertolucci-level, and that ceremony appeared, as well as snippets showing pieces of *Novecento*, the iconic movie that forced Bertolucci into the public consciousness. Other scenes also included past kills by Stellan, Gina, and even Fellini himself in conditions of grave danger and impossible physical skill. These film clips and video vignettes ended with the scene from the movie *2001: A Space Odyssey,* when the first human weapon turns into a spaceship.

Like a lightning flash, the screen went white and the scenery suddenly changed to a barren and beautiful landscape, identical to what you would find in Tierra del Fuego. There were vast valleys and riverbeds with mountains, but not much else around. There were few manmade resources, except a few rivers for fishing and perhaps a moose or elk to hunt. Players spawned in different locations, unaware of where they were in relation to one another. Their screens would flash a goal. That was the point where Fellini manipulated the outcome of the game. The power to give a different goal to a particular player would expose that person and cause them to be easily eliminated.

On all the players' screens, a goal written by Fellini appeared. All of the players had strategized this first match ahead of time and concluded that surviving the first stage was more about not engaging than doing so. If you chose to fire in an attempt to kill, or even if you succeeded in eliminating a player, you would become just as exposed of a target. Your probability of getting killed increased dramatically. However, if you waited out the majority of the round and battled the least number of times, then you had a greater chance of surviving. Of course, this psychology would make many players sitting ducks if they elected to retreat and hide. Noah was determined to succeed, but not by sitting on his hands and hiding. The goal appeared and he read it quickly—then he read it again.

To survive, you must reach the 65th meridian. Warning: you only have three rounds of ammunition.

Thank God I have a knife, Noah thought.

Only having three shots meant that he did not need to carry all the extra ammunition clips. Noah quickly discarded them to the side and began running in place, looking all around him with quick, thorough glances. Nothing anywhere. He needed to get his compass and map information to determine his location in relation to the 65th meridian. He ran to a nearby bush and crouched for cover, taking out his toolkit, from which he selected the map. His location was still north of the meridian. He needed to move south to get to safety. The good news was that his objective was clear. The bad news, however, was that to get south, he needed to cross an open valley and a river on the way to the mountain ridge. The meridian line ran along the foot of the mountains, a good fifteen clicks from his present location.

He began to sprint toward the river. He continued looking left and right, knowing that his movements kept him constantly exposed to any would-be sniper. He chose to zigzag, so that if he did become a target, he would probably avoid a lethal shot. At worst, he would be hit on the body. The bulletproof vest would make it a wound—not a kill. Then, he could force a one-on-one battle. The real danger was a headshot, but from a distance, the odds of hitting a moving, zigzagging target were low. On screen, his energy level was already beginning to wane slightly. Noah had to constantly search for sources of energy as well, and he was distinctly aware of the lack of food in this landscape.

***

Back in San Diego, his brother switched views and Noah's parents complained. He was just looking for opponents that might be able to threaten Noah88. He returned the screen to watch his brother playing, and the family continued cheering him on.

***

The computer screen allowed different views, and when Simon found Mark on the screen, he was happy to see that Slowpry was located away from most of the other players. One player was moving toward him, which was the most immediate problem. Before he communicated anything to Mark, he felt the presence of someone standing behind him. He turned around to find Director Stewart and a group of five coworkers. They had all worked with and knew Mark from other missions.

"Sir, I'm sorry about . . . sorry," Simon spoke apologetically as he straightened out his shirt and tie and kicked his coat further under his desk.

"Don't worry, Simon, we're all here for Mark. We want to make sure he's alright," Robert eased his worries.

"I was just about to make contact," Simon explained.

"Go ahead then," Robert ordered him.

Another CIA officer brought over a chair, and Robert sat down.

"This player here—Slowpry. That's Mark." Simon pointed to Mark's avatar, whose name was in blue letters.

"Slowpry?" Robert asked.

"It's a combination of our last names, sir. The name was available." Simon clicked on his tabletop microphone button and addressed Mark. "Mark, are you there? Do you read me?"

There was a brief pause before Mark's voice came in.

"Simon, I can," Mark said quietly.

"Mark, speak only when necessary. A player is flanking you from eight o'clock if you are facing south. Remember, you need to move south to safety, so use your compass," Simon said. His compass remark was a bit paternal, possibly condescending.

"I already did," Mark answered softly, but his tone sounded instantly aggravated by Simon.

"Sorry, just making sure. Move south and watch out for this player moving toward you. He's about a click away. Oh yeah. Also, lose the extra ammunition clips— they're empty," Simon finished.

"Thanks, Simon . . . good idea."

Simon sat back in his chair and began to observe the game board from a bird's-eye view. The action where Slowpry spawned was minimal. By now, most viewers were probably switching to where players had spawned closer to each other. Simon was happy that Mark received support from his co-workers at the office but was concerned about having the extra scrutiny of Director Stewart and his posse breathing down his neck. They might slow his thinking and impact Mark's chances or perhaps even jeopardize the entire mission.

***

Gina moved like a gazelle across the savannah. She powered her BlingBlingBaby so fast that she reached the edge of the river valley before any other player. If she continued south, she'd be exposed to sniper fire. She had to quickly decide what to do, so she stopped just shy of the edge. Gina was drenched in sweat from running in place on hard concrete while carrying all of her equipment. The heat in her shantytown room rose; she needed water.

BlingBlingBaby walked along the edge of the valley near the tree line rather than running toward the river and exposing herself. She found what she had been looking for, a small trickling tributary to the river that flowed with pure water. This tiny stream was a godsend. BlingBlingBaby knelt and drank by moving her avatar head directly into the water. On the screen, her health improved, and all of her yellow energy lines turned green. This water gave her some much-needed help.

Her avatar drank on-screen, while in her game room, she received a visit from a corporation worker that brought her a large bottle of cold drinking water. Gina took the bottle from the worker as though it was medicine from a nurse and began to chug. Water poured down her chest; the worker remained staring a moment longer than appropriate.

"What the hell are you doing?" Gina said in her heavy accent, dragging the worker's eyes from her breasts.
"Sorry, I . . . Leaving," the worker stuttered, embarrassed, before turning around and leaving the room. He began closing the door.
"Leave the door open. Get out of here."

The worker returned to his station in the hallway, where water and energy bars sat on a makeshift desk. He was in radio communication with the headquarters on the boat and was in charge of delivering these survival perks to the players as they found them in the game. That visit to BlingBlingBaby would be the highlight of his career at

Ultimatus; he knew that he would brag of having met the sweating champion in person for many years to come.

Gina shifted her concentration back to the game, ecstatic about the water; she needed the liquid as much as her avatar. She couldn't know for sure if she had gotten to the valley first. The danger of someone waiting to take a shot as she ran out of her cover had to be weighed. The 65th meridian was the goal and having had water early on gave her the confidence that she needed. She scanned the valley and found no evidence of tracks, so she decided to make a sprint for the goal. She took off from the tallest grass and ran with her head bowed down. Her avatar copied her posture, but her speed was still impressive. Her abs ached, but she knew that she was making good time.

Min's HappySpirit crouched nearby, waiting with her sniper rifle ready. She placed BlingBlingBaby in her crosshairs; maybe she could take her out, but the shot would expose her. Perhaps taking this shot was not the best strategy. Her hesitation wasted seconds and made the objective harder to hit. She changed her mind and instead ran after BlingBlingBaby. Min decided that the risk of a potential sniper was less than the danger in running close behind the best player in the world. HappySpirit was safe as long as BlingBlingBaby didn't sense her and turn around for a quick, easy kill. They ran south at pure sprint speed; the more distance they gained from the brush and tree line, the greater the payoff for Gina and Min. They were well ahead of every other player.

***

In the densest part of the forest, a group of eight players had been spawned in close proximity. Stellan's Firemist1 had spawned right smack in the midst of them; Fellini had sent him into a trap. He sensed the danger of being in a forest where tall trees blocked his view in every direction, and his instinct guided him to move up, not south. Firemist1 jumped and grabbed at a nearby tree branch and climbed expertly, like a monkey. He had only three shots and needed to use them wisely. From a short distance away, he heard movement among the forest shrubs—footsteps. He remained quiet and stared in the direction of the movement. A player walked into view, heading slowly away from him.

Stellan decided to kill silently and took out his knife. He stalked his first prey. Without hesitation, he moved fast, jumping from one tree to the other before dropping behind his quarry. The player had no chance against Firemist1. The first kill in the tournament was recorded as he attacked from behind and inserted his knife in the back of 8Alkemi. The player received a fatal blow, but still tried to turn and shoot at Firemist1. However, his fingers seized quickly from the kill—no shot was fired. These types of silent kills were common in the Ultimatus game but were rare in the tournaments. 8Alkemi was a first-time tournament invitee, which helped Stellan. Although this kill had been relatively easy, he was unusually stressed and was moving faster than usual.

***

In front of computers the world over, teens screamed and cheered for their hero, Firemist1. Some moved around their rooms, trying to replicate the moves that made him one of the ten best players in the world, if not the greatest.

***

Back inside the game, Firemist1 searched and removed the three bullets from the dead corpse's rifle by pressing his Ultisuit wrist button. A whirring sound started, the bullets lit up, and then moved to his

121

ammunition count on his lower-screen monitor of information. He had doubled his bullets to six, and his health was still perfect. Upon death, the player's corpse flashed its location for all players to view along with the current death count. This caused most players to move away from the kill, but Stellan had a new plan.

The monitor count on everyone's screen now flashed the number one. One dead player.

Stellan took out a small shovel from his toolkit and dug a shallow grave next to the dead player. He then lay down in the grave and moved the player over his own body. Stellan waited. The world's eyes were now on the forest. Most people were watching this, but none with more interest than Simon; he needed to help Mark in whatever way possible.

Mark was in a different sector, yet the entire office was glued to the location of the first kill, chitchatting about Firemist1. Simon switched back to Mark's area on the monitor, which brought an immediate rumble from the audience.

"Hey, what are you doing?" a CIA officer Simon didn't recognize asked him rudely.
"I need to monitor and help Mark, not watch the game," Simon answered.
"We need to set up another monitor," Director Stewart ordered to no one in particular.

A few nameless operatives scrambled another computer and its monitor from a nearby desk and proceeded to login. They chose the view of Stellan hiding under the body. They now had two views going simultaneously.

Stellan's strategy paid off. A new tournament player,

with an avatar named KevsTwo moved toward the body, looking to scavenge. He moved to the dead corpse and poked the head with his gun, looking for any sign of movement. Stellan had his gun cocked and ready beneath the body, but needed to surprise this player. He waited for the sound of whirring, as KevsTwo would at least check if there were bullets available. As soon as this sound began, Firemist1 moved his arm up slightly and pushed the head of the dead 8Alkemi to the side. He shot KevsTwo square in the chest. It had not been a lethal blow, but definitely a debilitating shot. KevsTwo fired back, hitting 8Alkemi in the stomach, thinking that he was the necessary target. He had still not seen Firemist1, and to his surprise, the disembodied hand moved again and shot him again in the same area. KevsTwo fell. He was alive, but seriously wounded; his hands and legs were unresponsive.

Back in his game room, Oscar Steenkamp, whose avatar was KevsTwo, struggled like mad in his Ultisuit, frustrated and helpless. On the screen before his eyes, he saw his death coming as Firemist1 rose from beneath 8Alkemi and put the kill shot square in his forehead.

The same fate had befallen 8Alkemi a few moments earlier. Oscar experienced his own death as his screen went black. He was enraged and disappointed, kneeling with his hands to his face in the agony of defeat. A moment later, Oscar felt something unexpected as his backpack grew incredibly hot. He grasped the pack, but felt no heat coming from the unit. KevsTwo, as he was known to the world, became physically paralyzed not from fear, but from the serum being injected by twelve small syringes into his back. The syringes delivered a fast-acting nerve agent, instantly spreading paralysis throughout the body. The player retained full consciousness, but had no ability to move. Within a few hours, the serum would work its way to the player's heart. The body, now paralyzed, was at the mercy of the corporation's leader:

Fellini.

***

Somewhere in South Africa, a foreign bank representative would be foreclosing on a gated community home in Pretoria to recuperate a loan. All of KevsTwo's assets that could be reverted to the corporation would do so, as per the terms and conditions of his contract. At that point, any connection to Ultimatus would be severed. No more paychecks would be deposited to the player's bank account, his Ultimatus employee number would be erased, and the avatar name would never again be used by anyone. His was an existence that had been shelved and erased. Only the data from his gaming remained available for Fellini's programmers, if they deemed it good enough to work into the next version of the game.

***

This time, Firemist1 did not stay to remove any bullets from KevsTwo. The next player coming this way would likely shoot from a distance, so he began to run. Stellan still had three bullets on his monitor. He found the best tree in sight to climb, but as he moved to jump to a low-hanging branch, a shot whizzed past him and crunched into the tree bark. Firemist1 was being sniped from behind; any player that had reached this level would not miss twice. He leaped forward and down, taking cover behind the very tree he'd sought to climb.

What's happening? Stellan thought, panicking slightly. *This is not normal. All these players so close. It's like I spawned in a trap.*

Stellan could not concentrate on the why; he had to deal with the reality of surviving the situation first.

Fellini had decided to eliminate Stellan, not because of Firemist1's game or fame, both of which helped Ultimatus, but rather because he had been sloppy enough to allow a GPS device to be planted on his body. If Interpol had gotten to him, he could be working for them.

***

Back at Langley, the cheering and backseat driving for Firemist1 resembled a teenage dorm room rather than the hub of a serious governmental operation. The game's new groupies were entertained by the action, but Simon was focused on directing Mark enough to keep him alive, at least until the next round. Getting Mark to the 65th meridian right away would not be a good idea. Simon quickly switched gears in his strategy.

"Mark? Come in." Simon shushed the other agents in the area, finally feeling like an authority to the others in the office.

"Here," Mark spoke in a hushed tone.

"Change of plans. I'm going to have you move away from all the other players. They're all moving south to the 65th meridian; I want you to go north-by-northeast and avoid them all. This direction will keep you away from all the other players."

"Okay, I'm moving north-by-northwest," Mark confirmed.

"Mark, I said east."

"I know."

Director Stewart was intrigued. Everyone supported Simon and Mark and seemed interested, but they weren't questioning Simon's plan.

"Simon?" Director Stewart said, a questioning note in his voice.

"Yes, sir."

"Why the change of plans? Why are you moving Mark away from everyone?"

"I want to give him enough distance so that he can take the Ultisuit off and leave his room to find out what happens to a player once they're killed," Simon explained.

"Won't Fellini figure out that he took off the Ultisuit?" Director Stewart fired quick questions at him, suddenly interested in micromanaging.

"We don't know. Removing the suit is a chance that we have to take. Slowpry, the avatar, will look motionless, but not any different than when a player is hiding. In normal gaming, you can leave the suit to go to the john or have a quick snack and hope that you aren't discovered. We all do it," Simon finished.

Some of the agents agreed with Simon and began voicing their opinions to Director Stewart, but he stopped them. From this commotion, he gathered that a lot of the agents in the CIA were gamers. The idea of an entire generation of new recruits that grew up playing computer games was quite strange to Stewart.

Meanwhile, Firemist1 crouched behind a tree, knowing that a new enemy was waiting for him to put a hole in his head.

He has taken one shot of three . . . Stellan counted in his head. *Let's see if you waste another one.*

Firemist1 grabbed the folding shovel from his kit and covered the blade with some leaves. He then moved the leafy object slowly, away from the cover of the tree trunk. A shot knocked the metal shovel out of Firemist1's hand.

You're down to one bullet, you sly bastard. Either you hit me in the head or you're dead. Stellan prepared for whatever was going to come next.

Firemist1 jumped to his side, rolling on the floor and pointing his rifle in the direction where the shot had come from. No shot came. His opponent was now aware that missing his third shot would mean being killed by Firemist1. In his scope, Firemist1 could see the trees and the bushes where the player probably hid; judging from the angle of the shots, the player was in the bush next to a tall, thick oak tree. He aimed where he suspected the player to be and took the shot. On screen, the number of dead moved up to three.

Stellan couldn't confirm the kill by seeing the flashing corpse as it had fallen out of view. Unsure of having killed his opponent he did not trust the computer confirmation, because someone somewhere else could have killed a player at the same time. He was experienced enough not to trust these unfortunate coincidences. He had to take a chance, though, so he moved in a rapid zigzag pattern to reach the bush, where he found BeauPP dead. He scavenged BeauPP's last bullet, which returned his load to three.

I haven't moved a click and already three players. Not normal at all, Stellan monologued to himself about the bizarre opening to this tournament.

All of this weapon firing recorded on other players' screens, making Firemist1 the resident of a "hot area." He decided to move north as fast as possible, even though it was technically away from the objective. He needed time to think and collect himself. He'd never been the first player to three kills; for some reason, he seemed to be the head that everyone wanted to bury a bullet in.

***

Noah88 ran hard until he arrived at the border of

the brush, where he clocked two figures in the distance, running fast. They were way beyond his sniper capabilities, and with only three bullets, attempting an improbable shot like that would be a rookie mistake. He sat down and decided to rest and plan.

BlingBlingBaby and HappySpirit will survive, Noah thought to himself.

Then, Noah88 noticed another player following them from much further back: SodaPop. It was the avatar of the funny Mexican, Ricardo Rodriguez. He was also a significant distance away—too far to risk exposure by trying to nail him with a sniper shot.

At least there will be females in the next level: Gina and Min! Noah reminded himself that he was still playing and that there were about twenty-five people trying to kill him. He had to process any and all information professionally, perhaps especially when it came to those women.

At that moment, five players, including Noah, stood at the tree line break in the geography. One of them was a Varda-level, repeat tournament champion: StealthUfo. Noah was in far greater danger than he had imagined. A single step forward out of his cover and Noah88 would cease to exist.

StealthUfo also noted the three players moving toward the 65th meridian, the two females ahead not pausing for any reason. StealthUfo concluded that the best strategy would be to hug the line and kill as many players as he could rather than making a run for the meridian. He began this process and moved east, hungry for his first kill.

***

On the screen back in San Diego, Noah's family realized something that Noah couldn't possibly have known. StealthUfo's presence scared all of them; he was only two players away from Noah. If he successfully killed Greca125, then Noah88 would be next on the kill list for StealthUfo. They looked in horror at the screen, screaming for Noah to do something to save his life.

***

As if the shouting somehow transcended time and space, Noah put his hastily formed plan into action. Noah88 cut long swaths of brush with his knife from the edge of the valley. He tied the tall, grassy material to his waist, legs, and arms using the ball of twine in his kit. The whole process took about two minutes. Meanwhile, as his name suggested, StealthUfo approached Greca125 without a sound. He proceeded to knife her in the side of the throat—an instant kill. Every player's screen now flashed the number four.

Noah88 dove into the brush in the valley and moved forward with only his elbows and knees. Considering that he was used to the carpeting in his apartment, the concrete floor of the tournament structure was very unpleasant, but his life depended on taking this action; Noah was not about to sit quietly and wait to be killed. If the cheering screams from his family had reached him from San Diego, then StealthUfo certainly would have noticed Noah88, but the camouflage worked like a charm. StealthUfo walked directly past the spot where Noah had been tucked away and continued his killing spree.

Noah calculated that he needed to gain half a click before being able to stand and run without much danger of a sniper getting a good shot off at him. With the screen at four dead, he had to remain crouched down. Moving forward felt like it took an eternity; five-hundred meters may as well have been twenty miles. At some point, the pain from moving this way would be intolerable, meaning that he would be forced to get up and run. He would need to decide this a bit later, but at the moment, he continued his three crawling steps per meter across the dirty concrete floor of his game room.

BlingBlingBaby and HappySpirit ran like the devil was behind them. Their feet moved so fast that their legs were a blur on-screen—the computer couldn't generate the image fast enough. They were on a soft slope up to the mountainside, and the 65th meridian was within sight. HappySpirit was coming closer and closer to BlingBlingBaby and the inevitable suddenly happened. BlingBlingBaby turned around and pointed her gun straight at HappySpirit's forehead. They stared each other down for a split second, but Min had planned for this moment. Instead of raising her gun, she put it down on the ground. Gina was satisfied with the instant surrender and put her gun away, turned around, and kept running. They both worked back up to a full run toward the 65th meridian. However, SodaPop had used their brief pause to narrow his distance to HappySpirit. When they resumed their mad dash to their destination, he fired a single, cracking shot.

The shot was aimed at her body, but the drag and distance caused it to strike HappySpirit squarely in her left thigh. BlingBlingBaby reached the 65th meridian and her screen flashed a brief safe-zone ceremony. BlingBlingBaby looked behind her and saw HappySpirit lying in the dust, writhing in pain. SodaPop moved toward her from a distance.

BlingBlingBaby was on the outside looking in, rendered inactive in the safe zone. She noticed this because she had no ammo to shoot with from behind the

65th meridian. Gina, as usual, tested the confines of the game. She exited the safety- line and her ammo immediately reappeared. SodaPop was only a dozen feet from where HappySpirit lay, prepared to make a final shot, but BlingBlingBaby was much faster. She planted bullets in Ricardo's chest and leg before his body hit the floor, his mobility completely disabled. BlingBlingBaby crossed the fifty feet to help HappySpirit up and helped her walk with a limping leg into the safety zone. The safe-zone ceremonies began on both their screens.

SodaPop remained lying there, immobilized. He was very much alive but feared that BlingBlingBaby would return to finish him off. He still had one bullet in his clip. He prepared himself to kill any player that got close to him. In the shantytown structure, Gina and Min were released from their Ultisuits. They were escorted down the hallways to the tunnel that led back to the comfort of the yacht, oblivious to the half-dozen players that had already been killed; they would simply never encounter those players again. Back in their respective rooms, Gina and Min both took showers and laid down to rest. They were thoroughly exhausted; running in place for the equivalent of a quarter- marathon was tiring business.

***

Mark was playing in a relatively calm state of mind, but it still made him nervous when he heard Simon's excited voice.

"I need you to somehow disable the camera looking at you from behind, hide, and take off the Ultisuit. You don't have any players nearby, so it will look like you're just resting or hiding. Go take a look at the room where Greca125, 8Alkemi, KevsTwo, or BeauPP played, and find out what happened to them," Simon instructed.

"Copy." Mark said quietly.

"Mark. Be careful, and be quick to return."

Mark grabbed his shirt and pulled the fabric out; holding the center of the shirt with his hand like a hose, he used his breakfast knife to cut the little bloom of fabric. It was a plastic knife, but it still had teeth to cut through the thin T-shirt. His shirt suddenly sported a roundish hole in the chest. He removed the Ultisuit as fast as he could, but left the suit parts extended in the same hiding position he had left on the screen. He turned and clambered up the wall, holding the top of the wood partition with one hand in the gap of space created by the corrugated ceiling; with his other hand, he placed the flap of shirt fabric over the camera, hoping that no one was paying attention to his feed.

Back in Fellini's control room, one of the four dozen monitors went black. Had Fellini been paying attention, he would've investigated, but he was locked on action developing elsewhere and didn't notice. Mark had to move fast. The camera on the flat monitor was used by the gaming computer to inform the program of the location of the Ultisuit sensors. That camera did not feed monitors for Fellini. Simon had thought long and hard about the technical set-up that was likely in place here, but remained unsure, half-expecting a guard to enter and shoot him at any moment.

Mark jumped out the window to the balcony and crept around the oval structure. At the first window after his, he found a live player in the throes of the game. Mark crouched and moved under the sill-line, past the window, and down to the next one. This stealthy movement seemed unnecessary, as the players were focused on nothing but their screens, but Mark did not want to take any chances, as the rear cameras in their rooms might show a portion of the window. He repeated this surveillance maneuver two more times, but he found the fourth room empty; the Ultisuit was lying there with no one around.

It might just be a bathroom break, Mark thought.

He took a chance and jumped in, hugging the wall with the monitor on it and hoping to be out of sight of both cameras. He wouldn't be able to disable the camera, however, and two units going down would create more suspicion.

I need to hide in plain sight . . . .

He dashed out to the inner corridor, verified that no one had spotted him, and briskly walked back into the room like a trained corporation employee. He picked up the Ultisuit and moved the system to the monitoring area, before moving back to the door where he came from. On screen, Mark appeared to be a worker tidying up. With that one quick move, he had enough time to investigate. He found needles sticking out of the backpack, along with small droplets of blood scattered on the floor and the Ultisuit itself.

So the players are killed right here in their Ultisuits once they lose . . . .

He walked back past the four rooms along the shorter path that the inside corridor provided. He reached his room, put on his Ultisuit as fast as he could, and leaped like a basketball player to take the piece of T-shirt fabric off the camera. He moved back to the main gaming area and sat on the floor to gather his thoughts. When Slowpry raised his eyes to the screen, he saw that a player was spawned precisely where he sat in that exact moment. The player was wielding a knife and clearly intended to bury it in his skull. Mark imagined that he could feel the pressure of those needles in his backpack.

"Mark, run!" Simon screamed in his ear.

Slowpry ignored the computer nerd from across the ocean. Instead, he moved his head and torso just enough to avoid the knife blow coming his way. He hugged the floor, dropping to a lunge position and threw his right leg around, hitting his opponent on the thighs and bringing him down to his level. Mark's adrenaline was pumping twice as hard now that he knew he carried lethal syringes on his back. Slowpry moved away from the player by back-flipping to his hands and all the way around to his feet. Mark made the exact same flip on the concrete floor, shifting from a lying position to a standing position with the grace and strength of a circus performer. Mid-flip, Slowpry had taken out his gun and now pointed it at the head of this player.

Mark had no idea that his opponent was Fellini himself! He had spawned a thirty-first player to investigate why Slowpry was moving the wrong way in the game; he wanted to quickly eliminate such blatant disregard for instructions. Slowpry didn't think twice before shooting him square in the face before running south.

Fellini was playing with his personal Ultisuit and entered a state that he did not like: shock. His triple playing screen went black and the death count switched to five. Fellini ignored Slowpry and instead focused on fixing the count problem created by his interference. He needed to eliminate two players. His office set-up, with its many screens, allowed him to sit and tap at multiple monitors that simultaneously accessed the game's core software.

Meanwhile, Mark sprinted south, away from the location where he had just put a round between Fellini's eyes. He couldn't remember seeing a name above the player's avatar. *How odd . . . .*

"Simon," Mark called his contact quietly.

"Yes, Mark. I'm here. That was amazing!" Simon gushed.

"Listen. The Ultisuit backpack is different here. This unit is equipped with syringes that inject some sort of poison or toxin, maybe a drug?"

"Are you sure?"

"I saw one that had been used; the player left behind some blood but no sign of a struggle. The syringes had done their work," Mark explained.

"Who was it?"

"No idea."

From behind Simon, as Mark explicated the situation, Robert barked out his instructions.

"Simon, tell Mark to abort. Immediately!" Robert ordered.

"Your orders are to abort the mission," Simon told Mark.

"But how? I can't exactly walk away. I'm in the middle of the Atlantic Ocean," Mark expressed, sounding irritated.

"Mark." Robert grabbed Simon's microphone. "You need to get out. You're in grave danger."

"Director, permission to speak frankly?" Mark asked.

"Of course, Mark."

"I think I'll be in even greater danger if I try to abort," Mark began. "I have no support and there are dozens, maybe hundreds of them here. I'm also unarmed. They're all carrying AK-47s."

"Fine, Mark. I understand. Just stay alive in the game, remove the backpack or disable the syringes somehow, and wait. We're on our way," Robert acquiesced.

"Yes, sir. I'll be here waiting for you," Mark signed

off.

"Over and out."

This confirmed Simon and Robert's greatest fears about Fellini. Mark was in grave danger playing a game that either harmed or killed the tournament players as they lost! Mark had to survive this round, but if he couldn't, then he had to at least do something about the backpack. Having those syringes dependent on the outcome of a computer game was far too intense to keep them dormant right behind his spine. Mark had a second, more ominous thought come to his mind.

What if Fellini can override the game and kill whomever he pleases?

"Get me Diaz in the Azores!" Robert Stewart ordered. "We need to get equipment and boots on the ground to that area as soon as possible."

"Director Stewart, I'm still waiting for Diaz to report on his surveillance pass. He's a bit . . . slow," Simon explained.

"I will see to it personally," Robert said.

"Sir, we have a carrier on the Atlantic about two-thousand clicks away. We need military clearance, so you'll need to speak to General Marshall at Rota. We're getting him on the line right now," an assistant spoke up from the back.

"That's still two days away, sir," Simon calculated and reported.

"We still need to deploy the ship," the assistant countered, "if you expect to have support."

"I'll be in deep shit deploying a full military vessel for a single operative. Stop the call to Marshall. We need to use the local option," Robert continued, working his way through the best options. "What's the nearest airstrip to Mark?"

"A small strip on the island, sir, but according to the

coordinates, it's on the other side of the island," Simon stated matter-of-factly.

"Sir," another assistant interrupted, "we have Diaz on the line."

"Diaz," Robert spoke harshly, getting straight to the point, "where are we on the surveillance job?"

"We're still a day out on that. Couldn't get the equipment." Diaz sounded apologetic, yet strangely casual, on the phone.

"My God, man! I have an operative whose life is at stake!" Robert shouted down the receiver. Everyone searched the monitors to find Mark. Slowpry was moving south, quite close to another player.

"Go further northwest," Simon spoke into the microphone, even though it was still in Robert's hand. "You need to put some distance between you and ProntoCall."

"I need a plane and a boat in Corvo immediately," Robert ordered, not interested in excuses or obstacles.

"Yes, sir. I'm on it," Diaz complied.

"When I say immediately, I mean immediately. Do you understand me?"

"Yes, sir." Diaz hung up and got to work.

***

The CIA team monitored two sections of the game, but they were not watching the area where Fellini spawned invisibly. He was near two players on trajectories that would converge in less than a minute. He waited patiently, allowing one to succeed in killing first. PsyIsGod was quicker than GuapoBen and drew faster, like in an Old West shoot-out, dropping him to the ground with a round through the throat.

The death count moved up to six.

Fellini paused the counting mechanism on one of

his monitors and shot the other player as fast as he could. PsyIsGod fell, even though he had technically won the encounter. All of this happened within a matter of seconds. To observers of the game, it seemed like the two players had killed each other, which would explain the kill count being at six. A shrewd observer would notice that the count had not registered both deaths, but Fellini counted on people counting up figures on the map and figuring that a glitch was catching up to reality. Fellini eyed StealthUfo moving on another screen; the cool killer approached another newbie, AldoMonti2, at the valley's edge. Fellini didn't need to wait long for the action; StealthUfo cleanly eliminated his prey, and the count moved to seven. Fellini pulled his avatar from the field, not wanting to give rise to suspicion from millions of viewers and bloggers watching every corner of the game.

Fellini always kept his interventions to a minimum. The last thing Ultimatus needed was for rumors of it being rigged to slip out. Any such suspicion would immediately push players around the world to change games. The count being at seven made the game move slower, not faster. As players died off, the probability of encounters diminished within the vast map. Also, the statistics of the game gave a clear picture of who was who. As players go, the better players tended to remain, at least in theory. A few anomalies had occasionally occurred in the past, but the first to go were normally the least qualified.

The players were all moving south; a few had begun to run to their goal through areas quite far from the action. One player had crossed the meridian near Ricardo's injured SodaPop, an easy target, but had avoided the risk and had run to the safety zone and the comfort of his cabin on the yacht. These runners were physically beat and didn't need to burden themselves with any more killing or danger. The stress of being in the forest with a potential fight to the death around every tree or shrub was mentally taxing, to say the least. Many players preferred physical exhaustion to mental stress in this survival game. To train a body for physical activity was simple; to have a mind trained to handle constant fight-or-flight decisions was another story.

Fellini controlled all activities within the ship and the game from his control room. He finished his count intervention and was back to overseeing the action. He kept Slowpry and Firemist1 on his two main screens. He was monitoring Slowpry because he had moved north rather than south, and he paid close attention to Firemist1 because of the earlier GPS issue. Fellini looked tired; he was sweating, and his face was a bit haggard. Running the complicated logistics and gaming challenges of the tournament was not easy. There were secret complex aspects to the whole operation that no corporation worker knew. Being the sole person in possession of the full game knowledge, coordinating the intricacies of the structural design of the mega-yacht compound, and monitoring the disposal of dead players was a stressful cocktail that had been mixed stronger each year.

He kept his control room locked. No one was allowed in unless he called them. He was manically obsessed with control, and control plus a photographic memory meant that anything out of its place would send him into a suspicious rage. The wealth that Ultimatus had generated for him, in addition to global success beyond his wildest dreams, had poisoned his mind against almost every other person he came in contact with— he was a roiling mass of paranoid energy, moving through life as though it were a game, pulling strings and cutting cords when and where he chose.

***

Director Stewart was furious that the Marines

couldn't reach Corvo with a military ship. Ultimatus did
not represent a threat to the US, so getting clearance was
very complicated. In any event, the US base at Rota, Spain
was too far away. Stewart was completely dependent on
Diaz's work in Punta Delgada. A few hours earlier, Mr.
Diaz had successfully commandeered a small Cessna and
was en route to Corvo. He was scheduled to land shortly.
Unfortunately, his departure had been delayed by
Portuguese red tape and pure laziness.

He had departed nearly two full hours after he hung
up with Director Stewart. Diaz flew over the Corvo
airport approximately four hours into the first day of the
tournament. He instructed the pilot to fly around the
entire island. The pilot wasn't wild about the idea, but did
so anyway. At 10 p.m., the visibility was quite low, and
given that the island was small and mostly uninhabited,
only the eastern face of the island had some illuminated
homes and roads. Lights also shone on the single pier
mooring where fishing boats and the ferry were docked.
Diaz did not find anything outstanding or unusual where
an international gaming tournament could possibly be
taking place.

The show must be taking place in the village, Diaz thought.

As the plane continued north and turned across the
western side of the island, he saw the structure. A strange,
brown, tin-roofed building was jutting into a small crevice
on a tiny peninsula at the far end of the island. From the
sky, the shantytown looked like a muddy barnacle attached
to a tiny cliff side. No road on land led to this cove. He
instructed the pilot to pass once more, but lower. On the
second pass, he couldn't detect any movement or life from
the strange metal and concrete compound, but his eyes
did sense a blue-green hue to the light around it, perhaps
something very faint. The dark night didn't help matters,
but the sky still held some receding summer light, which

could have been the source of this odd hue. He flew inland over the dormant volcano crater nearby. On the other side of the crater, the roundabout of the road's end coming from the village came into view. Diaz instructed the pilot to make an unscheduled landing.

Diaz decided to check out the brown structure. That strange dark mass was the only anomaly on Corvo; the tournament could be taking place inside. However, he needed a boat to get around the island. The only boats were fishing vessels and the Portuguese Coast Guard's Zodiac 750 cruiser. The conditions in the water, combined with the starless night, were too risky for the Coast Guard, and they refused. Apparently, on a new moon, pilot ships could not see the rocks. Diaz was told that he would have to wait till morning. Diaz checked himself in at the Comodoro, the only place in Corvo with decent rooms. He had just rested his head on the pillow, his mind whirring with thoughts and speculations, when he received a call from a desperate Director Stewart.

"I don't know if you understand the gravity of the situation. Diaz, we need to get to Corvo immediately," Robert practically pleaded.

"I am in Corvo, sir," Diaz replied.

"Have you made contact with Ultimatus? Have you found evidence of the tournament?"

"I flew over what I think could be the location of the tournament. It is inaccessible at this time of night. But we do have the coordinates."

"Diaz! We have had the coordinates for hours!" Robert shouted. What little patience he had was disappearing. "We need to extract our man, do you not understand that?"

"Yes, sir, I do. However, I am alone and will travel tomorrow morning with the Coast Guard. The location is not accessible by land," Diaz calmly explained.

"Diaz, wait for further instructions. Do not go

anywhere unless I tell you to." Robert hung up without saying goodbye.

Diaz was not pleased, but at least he had made his way to Corvo. He wouldn't appear totally out of it to his superiors if this all went horribly wrong. A stiff drink at the hotel bar would soften the situation.

Robert was visibly furious and Simon experienced some contact rage. They needed to fly support to Corvo ASAP. From the base at Rota, a Hercules aircraft was available, but the landing strip at Corvo was too short. They needed an Osprey, which could land on any field. However, again, the nearest one was in San Diego.

They were forced to use a small C-12 Huron that the Navy had at the base. The operation needed a good dozen trained black-ops agents and an experienced commander, but the C-12 only had a capacity of thirteen, including the crew. Robert spoke to General Marshall at Rota and explained the situation and their dire needs. Marshall had the Seals they would need, and the mission was underway by 3 a.m. Spanish time. The team would arrive in Corvo at approximately 5 a.m. and would then proceed by land and sea to the site. With any luck, they would arrive before Mark began the second round of the tournament. The timing would be close. Robert instructed Simon to call Diaz and ensure that he stand down with his Coast Guard plan. The last thing they needed was to tell Fellini that they were coming.

***

Fellini had heard the small Cessna plane flying low over the yacht during the middle of the first round. Their location was so far from civilization that any sound not made by a seal would put him on high alert. A plane at 10 p.m. in the northwest corner of Corvo was about as likely as finding Scarlett Johansson in a bar in Tierra del Fuego.

Someone brought a GPS, Fellini concluded. *This will need to be reconciled.*

Fellini began checking weather maps and directions. He would need to accomplish a great deal in a short time. This was the kind of stress that had shaped him into Fellini. Once again, he felt like a kid in a candy store. He needed a strong dose of his favorite dopamine rush. He needed to find the next logical move in the giant chess game of his own design.

***

Meanwhile, Stellan, certain that something strange was happening both inside and outside the game, moved Firemist1 south to the 65th meridian. He was lucky that Fellini was tending to other issues, leaving him unsupervised for a while. He climbed a large tree in the clearing that overlooked the valley. From above, Firemist1 detected the moving grass where Noah88 hid; he knew that it was a player. Noah88 was a fair distance away, which made the shot uncertain. Firemist1 elected to wait and left the unknown player to his own destiny. He needed to survive the match so that he could have a man-to-man talk with Fellini back on the yacht. He was almost certain that his GPS incident had something to do with this. He prepared his sniper rifle and began scoping the line between the brush and the valley's lip.

On the valley boundary, StealthUfo was closing in on the fourth player on the line, DarkGI. Five or six clicks away, other players had started to cross the valley, but they were barely specks, much too far for him to shoot. He moved through the brush skillfully, unnoticed by Firemist1, who was perched on a tree limb high above him.

143

StealthUfo could not have predicted what would happen next. DarkGI decided to make a headlong run for the 65th meridian. Firemist1 sensed DarkGI and put him in the crosshairs of his rifle scope. Firemist1 was about to take a shot when DarkGI fell dead, shot by StealthUfo. The death count climbed to eight on the screen, confirming what he had seen, although he hadn't pulled the trigger.

Firemist1 moved his scope slightly lower, and the crown of a player's head rose like a brown-haired moon in his scope. He took the shot and StealthUfo died. Stellan was instantly nauseous as the monitor flashed the name of his kill: StealthUfo.

His real name was Bernie Nuilly, one of Stellan's best friends in the game. The stress of having spawned surrounded by so many players had turned him into an instinctual killer. It was difficult to have friends in the video game world, but Bernie had been one of the few Stellan had ever found. The conversations he'd shared with StealthUfo would be missed, as well as the laughter over dinners and nostalgia about old tournaments.

Stellan closed his eyes for a moment and put that behind him, remembering that there was only one more kill before the second round, and if he didn't focus, he could end up being number ten. Firemist1 placed the crosshairs of his scope back on the patch of brush moving low along the ground, with Noah88 beneath it.

The count was at nine. Firemist1 had killed four. One more kill would mean that everyone could rest. The game had been going on for more than five hours, and all the players were exhausted, even Stellan. His finger caressed the trigger, and he adjusted the crosshairs a tad, moments away from planting a bullet inside Noah88 and bringing the first stage to a close.

The screen in front of Stellan's eyes changed and stopped the game. He hadn't taken the shot yet. All the players still standing were watching the screen flash a video ceremony. "Ten players have now been eliminated from Ultimatus," the screen announced, a wheat field in front of a sunset was the peaceful background image. Music that was befitting for the loss of friends began to play: Gorecki's Symphony no. 3, second movement. This was a victory and a burial ceremony. After a large heading with the words "Players Barred from Ultimatus," names scrolled on the screen in the order of their loss along with an image of their avatars and their highest level achieved:

8Alkemi - Tarkovsky
KevsTwo - Blomkamp
BeauPP - Haneke
Greca125 - Costa-Gavras
GuapoBen - Cuaron
PsyIsGod - Lee
AldoMonti2 - Bertolucci
DarkGI - Dembo
StealthUfo - Varda
MarissaB - Herzog

Noah survived, as did Ricardo. They were both lying in the valley, one crawling toward the river and the other wounded on the opposite side. Other players were still located in different parts of the map without much consequence, except for MarissaB, who happened to be killed by Nachomaster while hiding in the brush, waiting for the first round to elapse. Nachomaster's first kill in a tournament came because MarissaB forgot to check that her feet weren't sticking out from the bottom of a bush. It was truly the little things that mattered in this game.

Fellini needed to get into MarissaB's game room and remove her, just as he had with the other nine players. Fellini was furious for three reasons. The noise from the nearby airplane had thrown him into a panic, being killed by Mark in the game was simply humiliating, and having Stellan survive was a failure on his part. He made his move while the ceremonial burial video played on the gamers' and viewers' screens across the globe. Fellini went into MarissaB's room with the necessary sledge hammer, closed the door behind him, and removed the Ultisuit from MarissaB's toned and tanned body.

She was a player from Germany, but now she was a corpse that needed to be disposed of. Her family would miss her, as she had recently become a huge success. Fellini grabbed her legs and placed them between four barely noticeable holes on the concrete floor. He took two heavy-duty, plastic cable ties out of his pocket and inserted one through a tiny drilled hole. Fellini snaked the cord through and out of another hole, then around one of her ankles and zipped it hard. Fellini repeated this on the other ankle.

Marissa's body was tied to the floor. Fellini took the sledge hammer and slammed it hard on the floor between her legs. As if by magic, the concrete floor broke cleanly in half, but only a two-foot by three-foot piece of the floor fell in a prepared rectangle that had been made to collapse. The rectangle collapsed and pulled Marissa below to splash into the ocean. The body and the debris immediately disappeared. The concrete attached to her legs served as a weight and would keep her under the water until she was completely consumed by fish.

Fellini pulled a loose piece of concrete that lay in the

corner of the room, and pushed it to fit exactly in the space left by the hole. The edges were matching dado cuts, so it looked like the floor had been there all along. The piece of concrete was leaning in the corner of every room, but no one would have noticed it—in the shantytown, structural debris like that was everywhere.

Fellini walked toward the exit, but then remembered a detail that he had forgotten a few times before. He went back to the Ultisuit, grabbed the backpack portion, and pressed a concealed button on the back. The twelve syringes retracted with a sucking pop, leaving no evidence for employees of the company to see. Mystery was very important to Fellini; keeping people guessing about his methods, mad or not, was essential.

12

Fellini returned to his main office with the sledgehammer in hand, which he returned to a cabinet next to his desk. In this cabinet, he also had an AK-47 and a .357 Magnum, both loaded, as well as a crossbow with various types of bolts. He schemed and made decisions as he moved around the spacious office. He opted to make a change in his initial plans. Twenty minutes would be afforded to the remaining twenty players for showering, and then he would invite them to dinner in the main dining room. Mark, Noah, Stellan, Ricardo, and the rest of the players moved through the canvas bridge to the almost-forgotten luxury of their rooms. During this walk, their handlers repeatedly told them that they had twenty minutes before being expected in the dining room. Min and Gina, as well as a few other players that had reached the 65th meridian, were told of the dinner schedule via an announcement in their rooms. Ten other players from earlier that morning were no longer onboard.

Mark was unaware of the plane passing over the boat; surviving in the game while running recon missions on the side had been challenging enough. In his cabin, he removed the earpiece and the main device and returned them to their cases under the drawer.

He stood under a well-deserved shower for about ten minutes and then dressed and walked to the dining room. Meanwhile, Fellini readied some of his most trusted employees for a room-by-room search. He had all the players' rooms swept thoroughly with wands during dinner. Less than ten minutes into dinner, Fellini had the drawer with the shoe sole glued to its underside in his hands. He pried open the sole and peered in at the CIA device. The device was small and very sleek, the work of advanced technology laboratories that only a handful of countries had and Fellini strongly suspected it was the USA. Fellini took the main body, ignored the earpiece, and put the guts of the GPS communication element in his pocket. He replaced the cover and had his assistant return the drawer with the closed inner sole to the room. If his calculations were correct, Mark wouldn't realize what had happened until the following morning.

Fellini went to a corner of his office in the yacht where a spiral staircase led up to the bridge. He instructed the captain to prepare the yacht to move, but told him to wait until he gave the command to do so. He exited through a side door onto a tin roof below the window line. The captain on the bridge didn't expect this odd request, but would never question Fellini.

The bridge was hidden between the cheap roofs at different heights; the one above the entire bridge cantilevered, causing the yacht's windows to be covered when viewed from a distance. Fellini had to crouch to get past the cantilevered roof and onto a second roof where he could stand up straight. Perched high on top of the makeshift shanty town of rusty rooftops, he looked like the dark figure of a robber.

He jumped to the concrete terrace below the roof, a bit past the gaming room, and went around the terrace to the side where the boat was moored to the concrete pier extending from the cove. The geographic location protected the ship from the rough Atlantic Ocean wave patterns. He leaped down to the pier and walked calmly to its end. On land, he made sure that no one had noticed him on this barren and lifeless terrain.

Fellini cleaned the GPS with his Egyptian-cotton shirt from Harrods and placed the skin-colored CIA device ever so gently on a rock. He returned to find his sailors detaching the ropes that kept the *Ultimus II* attached to the pier. He boarded from the lower door, through which the sailors had accessed the lower portion of the pier. Some things had to be done personally; ensuring that the GPS device left his realm was one of them. The mere existence of the GPS on board the *Ultimus II* was a huge error that he wanted to correct immediately.

He reached the toy room of the boat, where his mini-sub and Jet Skis were stored, and called the bridge from an internal phone on the wall. The captain explained that the inflatable system beneath the concrete structure was ready—all they needed was his word. Fellini had designed the structure to withstand the need for a move such as this. In order for the boat to support the makeshift shantytown envelope surrounding it, he had added inflatable canvas bags beneath some of the bays that not only removed the weight, but also anchored the concrete so that it didn't bang against the side of the boat.

They departed and had less than eight hours before

the beginning of the next phase of the tournament. Whatever nation's Navy was in pursuit, they would have to begin their search after finding the GPS device, so he opted to leave it functioning and by leaving it in Corvo, not let them know about its discovery. He could have escorted Mark to land and left him there, but who would take his place in the tournament? His death online would also be a strong slap to what he suspected was the CIA.

Fellini's greatest concern now was the fate of the tin, wood, and concrete structure and how it could slow them down. The worst case scenario, of course, was a collapse of the gaming facility!

We had better move. We need a head start, Fellini thought.

During dinner, the players were all jolted when the ship began to move. Mark tried to hide his shock at the fact that the structure outside the boat was moving right along with it. He peered out the window, as all the other players did, and saw that the canvas bridge to the game rooms stayed in place. This disturbed a number of the players and Mark wanted more confirmation, so he went to the nearest window and slid the glass open. The concrete wall remained in front of it, and the tin roof stayed above their heads. Next to him, Stellan watched the same inexplicable event. They both confirmed that the water was moving slowly in the space between the boat and the concrete. A few yards ahead, they saw the inflated canvas bag pressing about twenty feet of the wall and the yacht. Water splashed up onto it, making for a noisy ride. The yacht moved slowly, but the *Ultimus II* was carrying the enormous structure along with it!

"Stellan, this is odd, right?" Mark asked, trying to mask any sound of panic in his voice.

"Yes," Stellan replied, similarly anxious.

"This is not right. This ship is not meant to carry this much weight. What the hell is happening?"

"A lot of things don't seem right this year," Stellan said ominously.

"What do you mean?"

"Well, first of all, I killed four players in less than three hours."

"What? You killed four players? That's unbelievable."

"Exactly." Stellan sat on the window seat and Mark did the same. "I spawned near half a dozen players. It was an almost impossible situation . . . I don't think it was an accident."

"What are you going to do?" Mark asked, intrigued by Stellan's openness.

"I'm going to meet him."

"Where?"

"Here, onboard," Stellan answered, pointing to the ceiling, toward the bridge and the master suite.

"You know that he's here?"

"I'm pretty sure."

"Well . . . good luck."

Stellan got up to leave the dining cabin and Mark stood, spontaneously choosing to follow him. At that moment, Gina approached them both, thwarting his nascent plan to get closer to Fellini.

"Hey, you guys," Gina greeted them.

"Hey, Gina," Mark said, hoping that they could simply pass by her.

"Hey, Puss Puss," Stellan greeted her in his Swedish way, but somehow colder than usual.

"I'm exhausted. I ran through the whole damn stage. I swear, tomorrow, I'm just going to sit and snipe all day."

Mark laughed and returned her smile, but Stellan, on

a mission, said goodnight and exited the dining cabin. Sensing that following him would be a strange move at that point, Mark stayed with Gina. He needed to follow Stellan but didn't want to arouse any more suspicion. Also, the opportunity to spend a bit more time with Gina beckoned.

"Have I ever told you how beautiful you are?" Mark said, speaking once again without thinking.

"No, but feel free," Gina cooed back.

"Well, you are. Beautiful, I mean."

"Well, thank you. I needed to hear that. I feel like a total wreck."

"I wish we could have met under different circumstances," Mark continued.

"Why? A luxurious yacht during one of the most elite tournaments in the world isn't good enough?"

"Funny, but no, it isn't. It would have been nice to get to know you without possibly needing to put you in my crosshairs tomorrow. The danger here is . . . intense."

Mark wanted to tell her about the needles that he'd found in the backpack but bit his tongue, his professionalism still protecting the operation.

"The danger? So what? You still believe all that garbage about the contract?" Gina asked him, smirking.

"It's being enforced." Mark tried to sound serious.

"Well, don't worry, I'll be fine," she replied with a laugh. "Not so sure about you though . . . ."

"Just don't get killed. I'll explain this all later, but just . . . don't die," Mark added emphatically, his face deadly grave.

"And what if we get matched?"

"I promise that I won't kill you," Mark instantly responded. He stared her right in the eyes. Gina sensed that he was being sincere, and she forced the emotion rising in her stomach down into the depths where it belonged.

Emotional attachment. Not here. Not now. These words flashed in her head.

"I need to go."

Gina turned on a dime and left the dining car, heading for her room.

The *Ultimus II* moved slowly, but as it reached rougher waters, the structure began to make more noise. Fellini counted on a maximum speed of fifteen knots, weather permitting, which would put them back in international waters in roughly thirteen hours. The advantage of night would give them the time they needed to get out of sight, past the horizon. Their direction would not be revealed. Whatever government was after them would be at a major disadvantage trying to catch up. Before they found a new lead to follow, they would be clear of Portuguese-controlled waters. Fellini had acted wisely by reacting so fast, but knowing that the government on their tail was most likely the US was a particular worry.

The tournament rules stated that the game would re-commence exactly eight hours after the end of the first round. The next stage of the tournament only required five kills to finish, so it would probably only last four to five hours. The rules only accounted for a short four-hour intermission before beginning the final stage. By Sunday night, the whole tournament would be over. Fellini would have to begin the second stage of the tournament while moving at fifteen knots—playing in moving rooms would be no easy feat. The connection to the satellite ViaSat-1 would be fine; Fellini had state-of-the-art technology for maintaining mobile Internet connectivity. Living on a yacht was no longer a way to escape. The world didn't allow those places anymore.

Fellini descended from the bridge into his office via the spiral staircase and walked toward the frantic knocking at his door.

"Open up, Fellini. I need to speak with you," Stellan shouted through the oak panels.
"Hold on . . . hold on."

Fellini spoke back from the other side of the room. As he went past his desk, he pushed a small, red button hidden beneath the drawer and moved to open the door.

"Come in, Stellan. What is going on?"
"I am, well . . . we are . . . I mean, what's going on?" Stellan asked as the noise from the yacht's massive cargo became increasingly unbearable. The creaking and cracking noises from the wind ripping across the tin roofs sounded like screaming in the night.

"We're moving."
"Why? And where?"
"Our location is not your concern, Stellan. You should go rest. You have a tournament to win tomorrow morning," Fellini spoke softly.
"Speaking of the tournament . . . why did I spawn in the middle of a trap?" Stellan asked.
"A trap? What are you talking about?"
"I'm not stupid, Fellini. I had to fight five opponents in three hours. That is *not* normal. I killed half the headcount!"
"Stellan. Stellan . . . you're the best player we have. You're here, aren't you? What are you complaining about? If the game is harder, so what?" Fellini spoke condescendingly. "It's clearly not too much for you."
"You know exactly what I'm talking about. If this is because of that GPS shit, I swear I had nothing to do with

that."

"What GPS shit?" Fellini lied with an impressively straight face.

"Please, Fellini. You can't fool me. You know everything that happens around you. I had nothing to do with that GPS device on me. I swear. How can I prove it to you?"

"Well, I do have one idea."

"Please. Anything. I'll do whatever you need."

Fellini then pushed the green button under his desk, which alerted his staff that he was safe. The guard at his door relaxed. In the next few minutes, Fellini hatched a plan to eliminate Mark, and Stellan was going to help him.

I will need her as well . . . Fellini thought. *But she can help me without me needing to tell her much. Stellan is a dead man.*

Below, dinner had ended and all the players were making their way back to their rooms. Mark could not bear the thought of having to wear the Ultisuit again. The stress of having imminent danger to his life in the syringe-filled backpack inches from his spine would paralyze him with fear. He needed something to prevent this danger. He searched the table and decided on a small oval-shaped silver tray beneath the water pitcher. He moved the pitcher off the tray and filled his glass, then placed the pitcher on the tablecloth. He surreptitiously slipped the tray to the edge of the table and dropped it on the floor. He crouched to tie his shoelace and slid the shiny tray under his shirt. No one seemed to notice.

***

Simon found himself exhausted, having skipped sleep for at least one night in a row—he'd lost track of the actual number. Director Stewart received a detailed explanation of the timing of the game. There was a twelve-hour gap before the second stage; Diaz was waiting for orders on the island of Corvo. Also, the air team would not be in place for a few hours. He ordered everyone involved to grab some rest. Nighttime in the Azores archipelago coincided with D.C. for five more hours; he ordered the entire staff to convene back at Langley at 0500.

Simon had an awful premonition as he went home to shower and sleep for a few hours. It felt like a part of him had been severed when he was unable to communicate with Mark. The hot, sticky August weather provided the worst "resting" environment of his short life. The soft pillow met Simon's head and he was out, but his body didn't seem to take any of the recharge that sleep always promised. He dreamt of being in the last stage of Ultimatus, helping Mark win the tournament. He had dreamt about being in Ultimatus plenty of times, just as many people around the world surely did. Some of the most eerie moments of his life had happened recently, in the earliest moments of the morning, when reality was still fragile and Ultimatus felt like real life.

In that particular night's dream, Simon stood next to Mark. They were looking at BlingBlingBaby as she ran past them. Simon noted how shapely her body was, even when sprinting. With Mark at his side they jumped in the water and began to swim. They both swam hard, but Simon kept glancing at the air above him, straight up at the sunny sky. Mark swam further down into the river water. The river became much deeper than he had expected, and he suddenly couldn't stop. Mark fell lower and lower into the dark water, and Simon continued paddling to grab him. Then, he realized that he had no air and needed to go back to the sky. When he looked up, he could only see darkness. He was drowning right along with Mark.

Simon woke up, sweating and terrified. The clock on his bedside table said 4:55 a.m. The alarm would have been a gentler wake-up call than the nightmare, but he needed to get back to Langley and get in touch with Mark. Simon had always regretted not having the physical attributes needed to be one of the great players, but most of his regrets centered on not being there with Mark.

***

The remote island of Corvo was not an ideal place to organize a team of US Special Forces for a rescue mission. Even getting a good cup of coffee was beyond the possibilities of the help. Commandeering the old Volvo station wagon of the hotel's owner was hard enough. Pedro Diaz was aware that the operation was an important moment of his career with the CIA. He was not able to survive on the wages he received from the agency, but he was lucky to have this unexpected subsidy.

He was all too conscious of his luck, or rather, his lack thereof, having been born in such a remote location. On that particular morning, he was awoken by a call from the kid in Virginia again and was given the arrival time of the US Special Forces plane. He rose and rushed to the airport, choosing to skip breakfast, something he never did.

Diaz was committed to helping with the extraction of the operative. He arrived at the tiny airport and went directly to the control tower, flashed his Portuguese Police badge at the guard, and ascended to the top. He was met by the man who was the air traffic controller, airport manager, and the highest-ranking officer at Corvo Airport working at that hour of the morning. He was also the only human in the control room of the tower.

"Good morning. I am Pedro Diaz of the Punta

Delgada Police Department. We have a situation," Mr. Diaz stated simply.

"You call this a *situation?* I call it an unauthorized landing in violation of our airspace!" Mr. Soleado shot back.

Mr. Soleado was pointing angrily at the US Beechcraft C-12 Huron parked on the airport tarmac.

"I'm expecting them."

"Fine, but they could be a bit more forthcoming. Do you know what they said to me?"

"Doesn't matter. Now, relax. I am here and they are with me. This is an Interpol matter. You will get your written orders in the morning. Right now, I am in charge." Diaz did not elaborate further. Soleado had a thermos bottle sitting on his counter; Diaz's eyes were drawn to it.

"Is this coffee?"

"Yes."

"Well, can I have a cup?"

"Help yourself," Soleado said, throwing his hands up in frustration.

"Thank you."

Diaz arrived beside the airplane on the tarmac with a disposable coffee cup in his hand, drinking as he walked. Before getting too close to the ten or twelve men dressed in black, he was approached by one armed US soldier that appeared to be guarding the rest. He identified himself with his CIA badge and was waved onward to meet with the commander of the Seal team.

The operative in charge of the team could not have been more than thirty. He introduced himself to Diaz as Number One. The rest of the men appeared even younger as Diaz scanned their green-, black-, and brown-streaked faces. They were all talking about either the mission or the game. Some of the Seals even talked about Firemist1's kills in the tournament.

Diaz outlined the two ways to reach the structure where he thought the competition was taking place: by sea with the Coast Guard boat that would be ready at 0600 or by land on the road to the volcano crater, followed by a two-click hike. They needed to split the team if they wanted to surround the compound and prevent anyone from escaping. Number One was not happy; he wanted to move immediately. He didn't seem to understand the rural, simple conditions of Corvo. They decided to give the Volvo to five of the men in the group. These five would map their way to the road that ended in the crater. When daylight broke, they would continue by foot to the rendezvous coordinates—the small peninsula on the north side of the island.

Mr. Diaz and the rest of the Seals would wait for the Coast Guard boat in the harbor. Mr. Diaz explained that the move to the harbor would be on foot.

"We're walking there?" Number One asked.
"Yes. The ocean is only a few blocks from here," Diaz answered casually.
"Well, great! So this is the kind of support we get. Walk!"
"Follow me."

Diaz ignored Number One's small temper tantrum and began to lead the way off the airport tarmac and onto a road leading to the port. Two full hours later, as daylight broke, Diaz and six US Seals were being driven by the sole Coast Guard officer in Corvo on the Zodiac 750. When they arrived at the peninsula, Diaz immediately stated that they were at the wrong location. He assumed that another peninsula further up the coast of the small island must exist.

"This is not it. There is another peninsula further up. Go on," Diaz ordered the Coast Guard captain.

"I know this island, sir. Your coordinates match. There isn't another peninsula on this area of the island." He pointed at the boat's GPS gizmo, which displayed the exact coordinates being sent by the GPS that they were tracking.

"Over there! It's a pier!"

A US Seal loudly shared as he pointed to the pier. It was built of concrete and blended in with the color of the rock formations in the background.

Diaz was shocked, to say the least. He had seen an entire shantytown here only a few hours ago. "What in the world . . . give me the GPS!" Diaz seized the tracking device and tapped on the screen, as though that was the secret to revealing the shantytown's true location. The land-side team appeared on top of the rocky bluff. Their presence confirmed that the location was correct, even if the miniature shantytown had disappeared. They all convened at the pier; all eyes were on Diaz.

Diaz followed the pinging screen to the rock where Fellini had left the tracking device. He picked up the GPS with a plastic bag and deposited it in his pocket. He used his cell phone to call Simon at Langley and explain the situation.

"Mr. Prince, I'm afraid we have some bad news," Diaz began nervously. Simon's stomach turned inside out. His premonition was playing out.

"What is it?"

"They're gone. The GPS is here, but there's no structure. No tournament . . . . Nothing."

"But the tournament starts in four hours," Simon

responded in disbelief.

"Well, not in Corvo. As I said, the GPS was sitting here on a rock. I can't believe this. I saw an entire structure here last night."

Mark is in real danger now.

"Okay. Find out where they went. Get a search party going," Simon ordered. "I need to speak to Director Stewart. Goodbye." Simon pushed his finger into the space where the phone's earpiece went and then dialed Robert without putting down the phone.

Robert was fast asleep as only a Director of Intelligence can be. Drugged. He answered, annoyed and seemingly distracted. After hearing the news, he told Simon to send a search team and meet him in the morning.

Little could be done at this point except hope that Mark had the training and skills needed to survive. A single Navy Seal against Ultimatus. The stakes had come to this.

13

Mark woke up in the morning, having rested just as badly as all the other players. The noise from the moving structure had tormented his slumber, constantly keeping him from deep, restful sleep. The alarm in his room had been set by the corporation and woke all the players one hour before the start of the tournament. The yacht, still moving, was pulling the structure along with it. He got dressed and pulled out the drawer to retrieve his communication device. He needed to alert Simon about the moving ship.

His fingers fumbled the secret compartment of the sole open and be blinked a few times at the empty space. His first thought was that he was still asleep and that this was some horrible nightmare. He tried to force himself awake and even slapped himself across the face.

Fellini knows. The device is gone. Mark entered fight-or-flight mode.

He looked everywhere, just in case he had made a mistake in his exhaustion of the day before. It was gone. He placed the stolen silver tray from the night before on his back and secured it in place with a bandage. All of the rooms had bandages and menthol cream for the inevitably sore muscles and joints of the players. Mark would be protected, provided he even got to the game. Fellini was in charge now; there was no way of telling what his next move would be. Mark needed to be on his toes.

To Mark's continual surprise, no one from the staff approached him during breakfast, nor before the tournament. Ready to kill at a moment's notice, he kept an eye on each employee, making sure that no one acted outwardly suspicious. His eyes also scanned for possible weapons. The guards had guns, but they were just stun guns in their jacket pockets. The guards also blended in with the hospitality staff, making it hard to determine who was security and who was simply delivering food. Gina moved closer to Mark and tried to make eye contact, but Mark avoided her. Mark was surely in Fellini's crosshairs; any contact with other players could endanger their lives. Being her enemy in the game was already difficult; he didn't want to be a threat to her in reality too. Gina was taken aback by his behavior, but her surprise soon shifted to anger, just as it always did when a man revealed his true nature.

To hell with him. Gina moved away from Mark.

Fellini was ignorant of Mark's foray out of the Ultisuit, so he was still counting on the syringe system to kill Mark while he was in the game. Using the Ultisuit to kill Mark was elegant and easy; everything was already in place to do the deed. Fellini had no need to rush Mark's death, as it would only make the situation more complicated and uncomfortable for the other players.

Ten minutes before the tournament was about to commence, the TV monitor in the living room turned on. Fellini delivered another speech to the twenty remaining players. The volume was turned up high to drown out the clanging noise of the yacht's movements.

"Dear Ultimatus finalists, the second round of the 5th Annual Ultimatus Tournament is about to begin. The eyes of the world are upon you once again. Please note that through the first hour of the tournament, you will be playing under challenging conditions, as this vessel will not slow down until we reach our destination. Do not worry, but I do not recommend going onto the balconies, as there are no railings. If you do go overboard, we will not be able to turn back for you. Stay in your rooms. This next phase will take place in a world that we have never mapped before. You will find that this new reality can have its . . . ups and downs, shall we say? Learn, adapt, and conquer. Good luck to you all."

Fellini was speaking live from his office on the yacht. After he finished his speech, he donned his own Ultisuit and prepared himself to manipulate the fates of the twenty players. A member of the staff opened the sliding door to the bridge; the noise of the outside structure grew even louder as the players exited the yacht and jockeyed past each other, pushing and even running to their assigned rooms. Eliminated players' rooms were chained and padlocked shut. The yacht's movement was sometimes jarring, but mostly rhythmic and consistent. Players at their level should be able to cope with this minor inconvenience. Mark stood to leave, but a guard approached him and spoke.

"Slowpry?"
"Yes."
"Please wait for all the other players to leave."

The guard gestured at another guard standing behind him; the second man was holding an AK-47.

***

Director Stewart and Simon were now in full panic mode. They needed to find Mark on a yacht somewhere in the vast Atlantic. The needle in a haystack cliché had never been more appropriate. Finding a boat actively trying to remain hidden would not be easy. They needed F-16s and an aircraft carrier to run sorties near the area in question. A cursory pass around Corvo to look for the wake of the ship had failed. For the time being, Mark was alone. Robert approved of, and Simon ordered, the necessary equipment to facilitate the daunting search operation.

***

Mark received a personal armed escort to his game room after all the other players had arrived in theirs. This time, the guard remained in the corridor by his door. Mark opted to keep his T-shirt on under the Ultisuit, knowing that there was a camera behind him. He had no option but to play and hope that the Seals could locate and rescue him in time. The yacht's movement compromised his balance, but all the players were in the same situation. His biggest handicap in the game was the metal tray, which forced him to keep his back unnaturally stiff and straight. A second handicap was his mind, which was flooded with the possible consequences of Fellini finding the GPS. The third handicap was the worry in his mind concerning the coverage of the tray. *Would one needle be enough to kill me? Two?*

The screen lit with the start screen and the following statement appeared. It was visible to both the players and viewers worldwide:

Players, you are the top twenty in the entire world. You are fighting to the death. Five of you will be eliminated; a four-hour rest period will then be granted before the final stage. Following that, our champions will be crowned and the tournament will be over. The first stage saw the loss of three-time champion StealthUfo, a Varda-level player responsible for many valuable improvements to Ultimatus. He will be sorely missed. Please, enjoy this next map and remember: play to win. ~Fellini

The screen flashed to black and then brightened; the players found themselves wearing space suits in a lunar landscape. Mark moved his hands in front of his face; on-screen, his hands were gloved as they would be in space. His buoyancy was drastically affected by the reduced gravity, and he used this ability to leap high into the air, both to scan the landscape from above and to test the environmental limitations. Descending took longer than he expected, which made the next stride a slightly slow process.

Lunar gravity. Pretty clever.

The players' goals appeared on their individual screens. No one knew whether each player had different missions, or if they were all moving toward a common goal.

To survive, you must find and board the space station. You have no weapons and enough air for four hours. Remember this: Pink is key.

Slowpry looked around at the barren lunar scape and saw no one nearby. He needed to figure out what Fellini meant. He could not see anything pink; in fact, he couldn't see anything but gray, black, and white in various shapes and tones. Mark's instinct was to move to higher ground. From there, he hoped that he could find the station. He moved to the nearest hill to use the higher elevation to his advantage.

Fellini had spawned Firemist1 on the other side of the hill, half a click from Slowpry. He expected them to collide within minutes. He also spawned random players nearby to make the odds of Mark's demise even greater.

Fellini let a small smile play across his face. *Stellan will get him.*

***

Slowpry and Firemist1 were indeed on a collision course. Back at Langley, Simon observed in stunned silence with Director Stewart and his entourage. More CIA officers had gathered at the monitor to share the fate of Mark. Palpable anticipation filled the room. Other players on the map were moving east as if drawn to the station. How could they know that the station was there?

"I've got it!" Simon screamed. "Pink like in *The Dark Side of the Moon.* Based on the location of the earth in the sky, the closest direction to the dark side of the moon is east. The base is in the east."

"But we can't tell Mark that," Robert reminded him.

"Yes. I know. Unfortunately," Simon said quietly. "You guys made a good team."

Back in the suburbs of Dallas, Mark's mother chose not to watch her only child's performance. Mrs. Sloan was a widow and had no knowledge of her son's secret life as an agent of the Central Intelligence Agency. She only participated in the life Mark elected to relate to her. In her mind, he was merely a good son who called his mother regularly.

***

Slowpry spotted Firemist1 as he approached him on the plateau atop the hill. They both turned in a 360-degree spin to see if the base was within sight. In the distance, a player was moving due east—moving fast. The only option was combat. Slowpry pushed forward with both legs and then swung his legs forward, trying to rock his position so that when he hit the ground again he would be able to repeat and increase his thrust even further. He tried to reach Firemist1 as fast as possible to deliver a stronger blow.

He hurled forward, but his calculation was completely wrong. His body careened into a somersault in mid-air, and he was powerless to stop his movement. Meanwhile, Firemist1 moved in a normal lunar walk toward Slowpry. He could see how powerless Slowpry was, but still cautiously moved toward him. Firemist1 calculated the best moment to strike.

Slowpry moved backward toward Firemist1, seemingly disoriented, unable to see what his opponent was doing below. He began to wave his arms frantically in a last-ditch effort to change his trajectory. Firemist1 calculated his angle of attack and pushed off the ground to strike Slowpry; both of his fists were aimed at his opponent's helmet. As Slowpry's head moved into a horizontal position, the helmet screen would be impacted by a double-fist punch and would burst. Then Slowpry would run out of air and be dead in minutes . . . seconds even. With a miraculously lucky break, Mark saw the reflection of the human projectile in the side of his helmet.

Slowpry reacted instantly and moved his arms in

169

front of his face a second before the blow landed. Firemist1 struck hard, but Mark's helmet did not break. The blow caused a physical reaction, and Slowpry was given more speed in the direction of his turn. His legs continued in their spin and struck Firemist1 in the stomach, pushing him away, while stopping Mark's uncontrolled spinning. Somehow, Slowpry ended up standing in mid-air, descending lightly to the ground. Firemist1 was not so lucky; his path smashed his back into the ground.

Slowpry walked toward Firemist1, who was on the ground, still getting his bearings. Stellan could see Slowpry approaching and struggled to get up. Seeing that his opponent was preparing to continue the fight, Mark decided to test something. He picked up a large lunar rock and hurled the projectile toward the rising Firemist1. The Swede did not expect this and failed to react in time. The rock struck his helmet glass hard and bounced away. It left a hairline crack behind, which slowly and steadily spread across the entire glass surface. Firemist1 would run out of air in minutes. Slowpry ran to Firemist1 and knelt down to speak to him.

"Stellan. Can you hear me?"
Stellan moved his head left and right.
"Take the Ultisuit off. Now . . ." Mark spoke again, but his voice could not be heard in the dead silence of space.

Stellan's Firemist1 knelt forward and dropped face-first, not even bracing himself with his hands. Mark wanted to vomit. He was responsible for Stellan receiving that deadly injection. He may as well have stuck the needles in himself.

I should have let him kill me. I have the tray, he doesn't.

He knew that staying to mourn would only result in his own death. With a heavy heart and a swimming head, he chose to follow the other player east. Simon, Robert, and the CIA staff members were celebrating Mark's survival.

In his private viewing area, Fellini watched Mark kill Firemist1, one of the finest players of all time. He was far from thrilled, but Stellan had to be eliminated anyway. He had to go deal with Stellan Boström's body quickly, but not before making a quick adjustment to the game. He sent a quick in-game text message to Gina.

"Stay where you are for five minutes if you want to survive. F."

That would make BlingBlingBaby stay in place a few moments longer, allowing Slowpry to catch up with her. Of course, to ensure that Slowpry would indeed meet BlingBlingBaby, he needed to figure out the hint about the station. Fellini sent another in-game text to Mark.

Pink. Floyd.

Mark immediately realized that the riddle was in reference to the album *The Dark Side of the Moon. Pink is key.* Mark looked at the sky and placed Earth in relation to his location. The nearest direction to the dark side of the moon was . . . east! He continued moving east, directly toward the waiting avatar of BlingBlingBaby, precisely as Fellini planned.

Noah88 was the first to reach the station. He had figured out the meaning of the clue right away; Pink Floyd was his father's favorite band. He moved as fast as his lunar movements could take him to the station, much to the delight of his on-looking parents thousands of miles away.

The yacht's movement slowed and then stopped; the rooms were no longer rocking. Noah was grateful; that added challenge had not been particularly pleasant. The removal of that annoying variable was almost more important than his impending fame, which he could practically taste. The problem was getting into the station. The door to the station was shut, but the keypad entry device had a note above it:

"Another brick."

Noah stood in front of the device thinking. It was another Pink Floyd reference.

Another brick in the wall . . . thought Noah. *The Wall.*

He entered the numbers 9255, which corresponded to *WALL,* on the keypad.

Nothing. Then he tried 8439255, which was *THEWALL.* Nothing.

Noah88 felt a strong tug that yanked him backward. ProntoCall had pulled him away from the station door, sending his body into a state of shock from the sensation of flight, but also because of the cord ProntoCall had removed on the rear of his suit. His screen flashed a countdown—one second at a time: Warning—you have 60 seconds of air remaining—Warning—you have 59 seconds of air remaining—Warning . . . . The timer continued lower, pushing Noah88 into a doomed spiral of fear and utter panic.

ProntoCall moved toward the door, but kept a wary eye on his first possible kill of the tournament. Noah88 needed air, but first he would need to eliminate his opponent to reenter the password. He had one more idea for the password, but no ideas on how to deal with the other two issues. He lunged forward with nothing to lose and pushed ProntoCall in the stomach with as much force as he could. ProntoCall was thrust to one side of the door and his suit cords became tangled on the metal-rod framework of the station. Noah88 had fifteen seconds of air remaining, as the warning screen continued to remind him. He reached the keypad and punched in 84309255 (THE0WALL), hoping that the zero would be equal to a space. The door rolled upward, sliding into a slit on the lunar station; Noah88 dashed inside. The door began to close a few seconds later, and ProntoCall decided to brace the door with his foot.

This proved to be a fatal choice by ProntoCall. His suit tore and the door smashed closed, despite his foot being in the way. He had to remove his exposed foot if he was to continue, but the door didn't relent. When ProntoCall finally pulled his leg back, he was already blue in the face. He died, still stuck to the side of the door, looking like a horror statue in a haunted house.

***

In San Diego, relief poured out of Noah's parents, who opened beers and celebrated their son's harrowing victory that had just been witnessed by millions of people. Noah's brother adjusted the computer view to the next possible battle, which would likely be soon. The master map showed areas where players' paths were likely to collide, and viewers could zoom in to those spots. He shifted the view. Noah's mom lost interest as soon as her son reached the ship and was safe. She didn't care to continue watching other players or the violence of the game. In the kitchen, she prepared food, but her brief respite of relief was short-lived. She soon began to worry about the final stage, which would likely commence late that night. Each successive game increased the probability of death for her son. She sensed this emotionally, not mathematically.

***

The screens of the world focused on Slowpry and BlingBlingBaby. Gina was unaware of the needles, and Mark seemed dismayed as she approached him. His inability to communicate the danger to Stellan pained him. How could he explain himself this time? He deeply regretted not telling her how dangerous the Ultisuit actually was. He allowed his emotions to rule him for the first time in the tournament.

In the work of a former Navy Seal turned CIA operative, coldness was king, but with Gina, different rules applied.

BlingBlingBaby moved toward him, but Slowpry didn't want to do anything too suspicious. He didn't want Fellini to suspect anything. As BlingBlingBaby attacked Slowpry, the logical move was to repeat what had worked before. Slowpry picked up a lunar rock and hurled the baseball-sized stone at BlingBlingBaby, missing her, on purpose, by a good two feet. Her blow struck him two seconds later. He fell back and stopped moving, even though the blow had not been lethal. BlingBlingBaby leaped into the air, aiming to fall on Slowpry's helmet glass.

Mark was looking at his monitor as the glass cracked and the counter began descending. He could have fought and caused some damage to BlingBlingBaby, but he wasn't about to cause any more harm to other innocently ignorant players. He opted to stare at her and lie motionless. Gina felt an instant sadness at killing Mark.

He was a decent opponent, but she had also grown

to like him. She would have liked to play against him in the future, but unfortunately, he would be banned from the game. Gina didn't believe that she actually killed her opponents. In her heart, she truly thought that all the players she eliminated in tournaments were somewhere at home, banned from returning to the arena, watching enviously. Maybe they even secretly returned with new avatar names. She refused to believe the urban legend that Ultimatus was played to the death.

Mark looked around the room, checking to see whether anyone from the corporation was moving in behind him. On the back of his Ultisuit, he felt the slight pressure of the tray being pushed against his back—the projecting needles had come out even though his oxygen hadn't run out. Fortunately, the silver tray worked perfectly. Mark was terrified by Fellini's treachery and the unknown future that players in his situation faced. Whatever was being injected into the players could not be good. Remembering what Simon had told him to do, he remained motionless on the floor.

In the tournament arena, Ricardo's SodaPop was running toward the station. In the station, Noah88 was looking at him and in full control of a lever that could open the door. Noah has been allowing free entry to any player that reached the station. The kill count was already at three and the game was only two hours into the stage. Noah had the option to leave players outside to die, but he didn't care; he wasn't about to have another inglorious death at the entry to the station. The constant presence of ProntoCall, frozen in terrified agony, was enough gore to be responsible for.

***

Fellini walked briskly to Mark's game room with his sledgehammer. He moved his arm, which instructed the guard to let him through and then ordered him to leave. Fellini proceeded with his gruesome routine. Mark was motionless, curious about what Fellini was doing. Between his eyelashes, he could tell that Fellini placed the sledgehammer on the floor and leaned the wooden handle against the flat monitor. Mark kept his eyes closed and felt Fellini's warm hands on his bare ankles, as well as a strong tug that repositioned him a few inches closer to the game owner. Mark heard the noise of the plastic tie moving through the concrete hole, but had no idea what it was. However, the moment the first zip tie tightened on his right ankle, Mark opened his eyes and kicked Fellini square in the jaw with his free leg, sending him straight to the ground—knocked out cold.

Mark had to remove the one secured zip tie before he could stand up, but this was not an easy task.

I need something sharp.

Mark removed his backpack Ultisuit and found the bent-up needles which had deployed onto the metal tray. He picked up the whole backpack and began to undercut the zip tie mechanism by inserting the fine needle backwards into the square holder. He was almost managing the entry of the needle in just the right way when he sensed that Fellini had regained consciousness. Fellini staggered to his feet, holding the sledgehammer over him. His hands slammed downward, but Mark easily avoided the wild swing and it smashed into the floor between his legs. It was as if Fellini hadn't seen him. *Is he blind?*

Fellini kept as much distance as possible between himself and Mark. He aimed at the concrete floor once again, as he had with all the earlier executions, striking the concrete near Slowpry's restrained leg. The concrete floor rectangle broke and Mark was pulled by the piece of floor still attached to his ankle, threatening to drag him down the hole. He struggled with his upper body to remain upright and then his work paid off. The zip tie was freed where the needle pressed the locking tab upward and the concrete slab splashed into the cove below. Mark threw himself back, away from the hole in the floor, only to find Fellini lining up another sledgehammer blow at his head. Mark turned away and down, avoiding the killing blow, but he still received a devastating strike to his upper ribs. He grabbed Fellini by one leg and pulled hard, causing him to lose his balance and fall. Fellini screamed, and a knocking on the door immediately sounded.

"Help! Help!" Fellini screamed.

Mark ran out the open window to the concrete balcony, leaving Fellini in the room. He barely had enough time to get out before the guards arrived inside to assist Fellini. Outside, Mark faced ocean all around him, there was no ship or island on which he could escape or hide. *Nowhere to swim to, nowhere to go.* The yacht was motionless, and Mark knew that Simon couldn't possibly have his coordinates any longer. Fellini had moved the ship away from the earlier location, without the functioning GPS. He needed to send a distress signal with his new location as soon as possible. He knew that a rescue was his only chance of survival at this point.

Mark considered his options during the seconds that he ran around the outside terrace, knowing that the guards would soon be after him. *The bridge. I can get a distress signal out from there.*

He moved toward the bridge, hoping to overpower whoever was tasked with guarding the entry.

In Mark's gaming room, Fellini regrouped and the tournament continued. Fellini ordered every guard to find

Mark and authorized the use of lethal force. Some of the security guards immediately went for the AK-47s stored in their cabins. Fellini went to his office and ordered a guard to remain at the door. He called the bridge and increased their alert level, telling them only what they needed to know. On the bridge, they locked all vulnerable access points.

***

Gina was still quite far from the station, and she knew that her four hours of air would soon be gone. She needed to run east and make it to the station or else go with plan B. Plan B meant ending the game by raising the kill count to five. She knew that Mark had hurled that lunar rock without intending to hit her, but his move had inspired a new strategy. *Hopefully this will work.* She picked up two lunar rocks about the size of tennis balls and began lunar jogging east, but skewed slightly north to try and locate other players. In the distance, a flash of someone showed up on her screen.

God, I hope it's not someone I like.

She took note of the kill count, which was still sitting at three, and wondered who else had died. BlingBlingBaby sped up as much as possible and reached the point where her opponent had no option but to turn back and confront her. She had already planned for this moment. Before he even completed his turn, she hurled the first lunar rock as hard as she could.

Hefner143 was struck at the nape of his neck, and the projectile passed straight through two life-support cables. The lines severed like paper. As BlingBlingBaby prepared to launch another rock, Hefner143 fell over, quickly losing his life-support systems. The count flashed up to four and almost immediately jumped to five.

BlingBlingBaby was saved by the bell, by none other than Fellini himself, who had decided to spawn and intervene once again. Uncomfortable with having the tournament and the search for Mark going on at the same time, he made an easy kill of a newbie called HappySpirit.

A second somber ceremony began on all the players' screens. Five avatars' names and levels scrolled to the now familiar "largo and lento" music:

> Firemist1 - Bergman
> Slowpry - Spielberg
> ProntoCall - Chaplin
> Hefner143 - Egoyan
> HappySpirit - Yimou

The fifteen remaining players were sent to their rooms. They were informed that food would be brought to them in their quarters. No interaction between players was allowed. None of them felt much like talking; it seemed like they had all simultaneously discovered that Santa Claus wasn't real and that there was no God.

Firemist1 had been killed. None of the players quite knew what to say, but all of them were eager to find out who had slain one of the gaming idols of the world.

Fellini sent strict orders down to the staff, and they promptly shushed and chastised the few players conversing on the way to their rooms. Players were told in no uncertain terms that no one was to leave their room until further notice.

Gina searched for Mark in the dwindling crowd, but only spotted Noah and Ricardo behind her. They stared at her blankly, shrugging their shoulders and making disgusted faces at the shift in atmosphere that the tournament had suddenly taken.

14

Mark tried to enter the bridge, but from the outside, it was totally impossible. All yacht entries were closed, but he desperately needed to get inside somehow. He realized the competition was on break, but he couldn't join the players going back into the yacht through the main canvas bridge. He moved lower than the players' rooms, down to the guts of the structure, which had no floor, only concrete trusses between posts.

The bedroom windows faced the small space between the yacht and the concrete wall, which varied in width, but was roughly three feet wide. With the yacht stopped, the ocean beneath the structure was calm. Mark dove into the Atlantic Ocean and ducked beneath the concrete wall to the inside wall of the ship. He propped himself between the wall and the concrete, moving up gradually by pressing his body against both sides. He reached the porthole window in Min's room, but she wasn't there. He knocked a few times but received no response.

Maybe she's in the shower, Mark rationalized hopefully.

He moved up to the next level with more difficulty; the slippery yacht wall proved hard to brace against, and his strength was beginning to wane after his recent days of exhaustive activity. At the next level, the window was far larger, and pure chance placed Gina's room directly above Min's.

Mark had no choice; she had killed him in the game, but being that this was her fourth tournament, and a Visconti level player, she probably knew Fellini. How deep her involvement went in Ultimatus was still unknown. He knocked on the glass, and Gina jumped up in shock. She knew that players didn't die in real life because of the game. Seeing Mark again confirmed her theory, particularly because she had been the player to kill him.

Gina opened the window and Mark crawled in, silently sliding the glass closed behind him. He immediately made the international symbol for silence with his index finger to his lips. With a simple hand gesture, he beckoned her into the bathroom, where he opened the faucet and turned on the shower to cover the sound of his voice.

"Gina. Listen to me carefully. Fellini is a killer. If you lose in the game, the Ultisuit kills you," Mark began in a rush, covering the important things first.

"But I killed you . . . ."

"I had protection." Mark knew that would be her first reaction. He showed her the tray still attached to his back held by bandages around his torso. He was in pain from Fellini's sledgehammer and took care to remove the bandages. No blood was apparent but the blow left a serious black and blue mark. He dried himself with care not to hurt that area and Gina gently dried the hurt area.

"Here let me put Arnica gel on it." Gina said.

"Thanks." Mark sat on the toilet seat and noticed how elegant the marble and the details of her room where.

"The Ultisuit backpack is embedded with needles that release some sort of toxin. If you lose, you die. You have to believe me." He began.

"But if that is so, then they know you escaped."

"Yes."

"But it will be OK. Right. If the computer failed to kill you they won't do it in person."

"I am afraid it is a little more serious than that. I work for the CIA," Mark finished, somewhat burying the lead.

"The CIA? What?"

"You can't play the final stage."

"But, but . . . Min . . . and . . . ."

"Listen, Gina. If you decide to play, then please, at least put this on your back. It's the only way I thought of to survive if you're killed in the game."

"I can't believe this!"

"I have to go. I need to get to the bridge and send a distress signal." Her words finally caught up to him. "Wait, what about Min?"

Gina stared into the eyes of the kind of man she had always wanted to be with.

"Min . . . was killed . . . in the last stage . . . she was number five." Gina struggled to put it into words.

The sinking feeling of real death was beginning to

affect her emotions. Hearing that Min had been eliminated struck Mark like Fellini's sledgehammer. He had truly liked her; the finality of death was much harder to consider when he knew the person. He felt a similar pain when he thought of Stellan, whom he had personally eliminated from the game—and from life.

"I have to get out of here before I compromise your safety," Mark said, holding her shoulders with two hands. He pulled her toward him and kissed her, hard and long. He pulled away and locked eyes with her for a moment. More important things needed to be said, but there would hopefully be time for that later.

"Gina, stick your head out the door, and tell me if there are any guards."

Gina casually opened her door and peeked into the corridor. There was a guard at the very end, looking in the opposite direction.

"One. Down at the far end of the hall. He's looking away though."
"Okay. Goodbye. Stay safe. Use the tray. It limits your movement, but it saved my life."

Mark kissed her again and quietly stepped out and walked in the other direction. He pulled the door shut.

"I'm mad at you," Gina said to the door, the only rational statement she could make given the massive amount of emotions and thoughts that now swept through her mind.

Mark tiptoed away, ensuring that if seen, the guard would not be able to tell which room he had left. He was thinking of his safety as well as hers. Mark went up the stairs at the end of the hallway, relieved that his presence had gone unnoticed thus far. At the next level, he could hear a commotion of some kind. Guards were moving fast along the hallways; orders were being given left and right. Mark needed a weapon and the glass-enclosed fire extinguisher and axe on the other side of the hall looked like his best bet. That was his next move.

The hallway grew quieter a few moments later, and he moved cautiously up to the landing. Just as he arrived, a guard turned on the stairs, oblivious to Mark who punched him in the gut with all his might. Unprepared to receive the blow, the guard crumpled down the stairs. Mark knew that the thump at the bottom would surely alert the guard in the hallway below, so Mark moved up to the fire compartment, broke the glass with his knee, and removed the axe.

Mark was still far from the bridge but was determined to access the communication equipment at any cost. He ran full speed down the hall and up the next staircase. As he turned into the stairs, a guard coming up from a lower level caught a glimpse of him and called over the walkie-talkie, alerting all of the guards to Mark's exact location. Mark approached the closed bridge door and saw no other option but to smash the lock with the butt of the axe. The door opened before his blow even began and he found himself facing two guards with AK-47s already in the position to shoot. He looked behind him to find guards on either side of the hallway, also with guns drawn. He knew when he had no options; perhaps he would live to fight another day. Mark dropped the axe and raised his arms.

***

Mark was taken to Fellini's office on the ship. His hands were tied with plastic zip ties, identical to those used to tie the eliminated players to their concrete weights.

Fellini had been confident that the poison in the Ultisuit always worked and was not happy to find Slowpry apparently alive and well.

The office was a square room, but the monitors were placed in a 360-degree circle around a circular desk with a small hole in its center to enter and exit. Within the thick desk, a straight, narrow hallway led to the center hole, like a donut with a single bite taken through to its core. The yacht design was modern and minimalist in the office, but the marble-slab floors in bookmatch joinery and the birdseye maple furniture was fitting for the outstanding wealth of his captor.

Fellini was looking at the computer stats of Slowpry on the main screen, seeing how he had improved the code since he began. Fellini was obsessed with entering new parameters into the computer and making Ultimatus ever better, even in the midst of a crisis. Computers can never beat the instincts of a human, but Fellini's game managed to record the strategy of the most amazing minds in gaming history. Today, he would extract and insert the code of moves made by Slowpry, who had been the fastest new player to ever reach the tournament. On the computer screen, the reflection of Mark's body shaded the code, that Fellini was working on. He turned around slowly, as though he had all the time in the world.

Mark had been trained to identify physical attributes, and he was trying to size up Fellini in the brief instant before their interaction actually began.

His first impression was that of a white man in his early forties with a slim body, about six feet tall. He appeared well-groomed and superficially wealthy. He was Caucasian but not specific to any particular region. He could be a good-looking Greek, Italian, German, Spanish, Argentinian, Chilean . . . anything. Yet he gave off a strange aura of the Mediterranean, northern Italy, perhaps? It was a mystery.

"Finally, I get to meet the fastest gamer to reach the tournament," Fellini said with mock praise.

"That's your take on all of this?" Mark replied incredulously.

"I care about Ultimatus."

"What matters is that your evil operation is ending."

"Evil?"

"You know exactly what I mean."

"Actually, I don't."

"You're a murderer, Fellini, or whatever your real name actually is. Do I detect an accent?"

"I don't know, do you? I don't really care, but you seem to have an accent yourself. Northern Texas? Dallas?"

Mark stared at Fellini, trying to maintain a good poker face. He didn't like to be less informed than his opponent. In this arena, he was already losing that battle.

"I used a normal name a long time ago, but that life is over. I control and own the most successful gaming corporation in the world. Perhaps you're not aware of who you're dealing with. No laws have been broken here," Fellini added with a malicious sneer.

"You bring people here to die."

"Oh, how wrong you are, Slowpry. I bring them here to live. They come here and play under the full consequences, as they each agreed to, even you. Through them, I am able to develop the best computer gaming code of any game on the market. I also pay them very well—when they win, of course. Millions of euros . . . or should I say dollars. C." He paused. "I." He paused again. "A."

"You're completely insane!" Mark interrupted, losing his cool and raising his voice.

"Insane? How is this business proposition different than so many others in our society? Boxers get millions of dollars for their physical abilities, but when they collapse, die suddenly, or live a life of mental disorder, society accepts this as the natural order of things. People pay to watch others put themselves in danger—no one watches NASCAR because they're hoping there *won't* be a crash. They are all hoping to witness something dramatic . . . a terrible accident . . . the death of a star. People look for the deadliest show they can find. Period. Consumers are immoral; online, only death and sex sell. I chose a business that embraces the consequences of our passions. Business is not about morality or sentiment. It's about money and fame."

Fellini was right. Why was an extreme sport exempt from endangering the lives of children? A disclaimer form? Well, Ultimatus had a lengthy one.

In Fellini's mind, no one could fight progress . . . Orwell was right. Corporations were the new superpowers, and countries were willing to create alliances based on money alone.

"Our gamers die because they get lazy," Fellini continued his verbal manifesto. "They stop evolving into better players and their skills become obsolete. When they are no longer competitive, they die. They're aware of this and yet they come back. They can stop anytime they desire, except when they are in the tournament. They all know this yet they still come, because we are giving them a chance that so few will ever have."

"But they don't really think that they'll die!" Mark said. "Don't you understand?"

"Are you so sure? I think that you are the one who doesn't understand. The full consequences contract is impeccably clear."

"Even if they do understand, you still have no right

to kill them. You're playing God!" Mark was trying to reason with a madman.

"All societies are tiered. Do you think the average Joe in America has any say in what his government does? Or that the President is ever in any danger when he begins a brutal war? Don't you think the deck is stacked in favor of those who make and deal the cards? This is why the best players in Ultimatus are millionaires. They contribute the best code and the most innovative moves, so they survive year after year. Gina's been here three years in a row. Why is she able to make it back again and again? Because she knows that the real objective of the game is to come back—to survive. Every year that she does, she is one million euros richer."

"But you're killing three humans for each Gina that you find!"

"And? It's called collateral damage. I'm making the best game that the world will ever see. I'm creating the highest level of entertainment technology. Everyone loves to watch. The promise of making money—big money—makes participation all the more compelling."

"You're insane," Mark stated harshly.

During Fellini's monologue, Mark had been working on surreptitiously loosening the plastic ties on his hands.

"Stop calling me insane, Mr. Prince. Your real name is Prince, yes? Simon Prince?" Fellini knew something was wrong in his gut; things weren't quite working out. Unused to being in this situation, even as his thoughts were developing, he brainstormed.

This can't be Simon Prince . . . .

Fellini realized that this man could not be from New England, as he knew Prince was—not with that Texan twang . . . .

"You couldn't rise this fast alone. Who are you? Where is Mr. Prince?"

"I'm Mark Sloan, and yes, I'm from the CIA. Mr. Prince is back in Langley, presently organizing your capture."

"So, there were two of you. No wonder you rose so quickly."

"Just as fast as you're going to fall," Mark quipped.

"You have a quick tongue. But as we say back home: barking dogs don't bite. Do you have any idea how many people depend on this corporation? Do you know how hard it is to create a marketing success as I have? Furthermore, once it starts, do you know how hard it is to stop? Do you have any idea how this corporation has evolved now that it is a global success?"

"You don't run a true marketing success; you're cheating at the top and killing the best paid players."

"Are you surprised?" Fellini said. "How is this any different from firing an overpaid board of directors?"

"*Firing.* Not killing. You like playing God, deciding who lives and who dies. Moreover, you have the incentive to kill your idols and get the money back."

"I don't kill them, Mr. Sloan. They lose in battle to other players. I am not a cheap man."

"That's not much comfort to the dead. Nor to their families."

"Not unlike those cheated out of money by financial scams or potentially thrilling athletic careers by a broken limb. I can't feel responsible for their suffering," Fellini said.

"You know that my agency is looking for me. How do you intend to get away from the most powerful intelligence agency on the planet?"

"Do you really think that they can find us? Or that they'll even try? They saw you die on screen. Slowpry is gone. You surely told them the seriousness of the tournament by now; my guess is that they'll write you off. Just like Ultimatus does with its dead players. You did sign a contract with them, right? You understood that you could die in service to your country, didn't you?"

"Yes."

"You read those terms and conditions, didn't you?"

"Yes. But, it's different . . . that's serving a country," Mark stumbled in his argument, not expecting this madman to be so articulate.

"It's not different, Mark. The players signed; they are consenting adults. If they die, then they were conscious of the risk. Our terms are written just like your foolish, patriotic contract—both of which are now partially costing you your life."

"The US will find this ship and sink it to the bottom of the ocean. Mark my words," Mark threatened, somewhat emptily.

Fellini laughed.

"They will stop you. And they'll shut down the game," Mark continued, trying to keep his voice from sounding desperate.

"You can kill me, but you won't stop the game," Fellini said, still snickering. "You can even sink this ship and you won't stop the game. Do you think the game lives here or something? Do you think that my yacht's little computers run something at that scale? If so, then perhaps Mr. Prince has been pulling *all* your strings . . . even the ones on your brain."

"Where is the server?" Mark asked.

"If there was only one, I certainly wouldn't tell you, but Ultimatus is a far greater program than that. I'll explain, my friend, because you're already a walking, talking corpse. This game is a series of packets of code constantly connecting between computers; there are many copies of the same parts . . . many, many copies. If one packet is missing, the game instantly accesses another identical packet from somewhere else."

"So how many servers are there?" Mark asked, getting close to slipping a hand free from the plastic ties. A guard grabbed his wrists from behind and placed another tie and zipped it hard, ruining whatever hope Mark had of freeing himself.

"Good. Thank you. Now, Mark, let me show you something."

Fellini turned to his computer. He pressed a few keys, and a program he clicked ran a quick flash presentation. It consisted of a line connecting two large cities, but then morphed into a map like those used to portray airline routes. The red lines ran between all the cities in the world, and then multiplied like a virus to join with all the towns, splitting again to reach all the remote areas. Eventually, there were so many red lines that the entire screen pulsed like a pool of blood.

"The software lives in the users' computers," Fellini said proudly.
"What?"
"You heard me, Mr. Sloan. See? You cannot *stop* the game."

Mark was in absolute shock. Fellini had beaten him at every turn. His vision of red lines faded to black as a strong blow to the head sent him falling into darkness.

15

Gina prepared her body with the tray from Mark before heading to the last stage of the tournament, wrapping the bandage around her breasts and back. The four hours between stages had gone by fast, and Gina had not rested at all. She was a nervous wreck. The hallways were cleared, and all the players were summoned to the living room thirty minutes early. On the way up, food and water were provided, and some of the remaining players ate quickly. Gina sat down and mindlessly chewed through an apple and drank some water. The reunion of competitors was no longer festive. Most of the remaining players were level-nine repeat winners, with the notable absence of Stellan, StealthUfo, and ProntoCall.

Gina had a hole in her gut from mourning the actual death of so many she had killed in past tournaments. Waves of guilt and loss were making her unsteady. She was torn with the desire to tell everyone to stop playing . . . to stop this insanity. She eventually noticed what the other players had obviously clocked, which was probably the source of the overall low mood: their guards all held AK-47s and looked meaner and more menacing than ever. They were everywhere, and their presence seemed to promote a heavy silence—a separation. Gina missed Firemist1, HappySpirit, and Slowpry . . . especially Slowpry.

Gina kept her eyes on the guards or anyone from the company that might give her some clue as to Mark's whereabouts. So much suspicion and strangeness made the air feel thick.

At least she wouldn't die in the tournament if she lost in the game. But who knew what would happen to her if she lost and then the guards found her alive . . . would they hunt her down the way they had with Mark? Probably. The *Ultimus II*'s location in the middle of the Atlantic Ocean also unsettled her.

This is not what I expected my weekend to be, Gina thought.

The screen in the living room flickered to life, and Fellini made his third and final appearance. He spoke in a different tone; he was more serious than ever before.

"Finalists, you have arrived at the apex of your Ultimatus career. This has been a rare tournament; three of our prior champions have been eliminated: Firemist1, our all-time champion with four completed tournaments and the highest scores ever; StealthUfo, with more kills per game than any other competitor; and ProntoCall, who became a repeat champion just this year. None of those great competitors will ever be able to play Ultimatus again. The game will truly miss them."

There he goes with his cryptic language. Why doesn't he just say what really happened. They're DEAD, Gina wanted to scream at the screen.

"There will be a special final stage in our worldwide Ultimatus Tournament this year. We had an anomaly in the last game, and a player that had been recorded as dead did not actually die. Slowpry will be a participant in the final stage. This means that there will be sixteen players, not fifteen, so when six players are eliminated, the ten new finalists will be announced. This year, they will each be paid a guaranteed one million euros. They will also be permitted to engage in speaking conferences and endorsements—something that Ultimatus has never allowed in the past."

"Players that have been banned will still be banned. Perhaps in the future, with incoming advanced identity software recognition, banned players may be able to return after penalty time limits, but that is not the case today. Now, let the final stage begin. Please proceed to your game rooms. And, as always . . . . Learn, adapt, and conquer. Good luck to you all."

***

Mark awakened in the room where he had played before. He was reeling from pain and rubbed his screaming head with his hands. An AK-47-wielding guard was standing above him, pointing at the Ultisuit. Mark was forced into the suit by another guard, and he felt the backpack portion of the Ultisuit pressed against his bare skin, ready to deploy the syringes into him at any time.

Behind the computer monitor, Fellini could override his controls and kill him with a single push of a button.

Just like when someone controls the payouts of a poker website, Mark thought cynically.

Online gambling is a hoax; Ultimatus is also a hoax. And this Fellini guy is a fucking nut. Mark began thinking hard. The Ultisuit had to function as a Bluetooth device, and the transponder probably came from the monitor-eye directly in front of him. If he kicked the screen hard enough, he might disable the Ultisuit before the injections were activated. He would have to move fast; unfortunately no one could move faster than an AK-47 round. *Bad idea.*

The screen turned on and the game began. Much of the online world was watching the same screen. Fellini added a final message:

"Players, you are the best sixteen players in the world. I say sixteen because the computer program at Ultimatus granted Slowpry a new opportunity to live. Slowpry was killed by BlingBlingBaby in the last stage, but the computer extracted him too early. We determined that he had enough air to survive and have thus given him a final chance. Six of you will be eliminated, and then the ten best players in the world will be crowned. Enjoy this final map, and play to win! ~Fellini."

The screen started to populate a new world in dim light; a purple-blue hue hung over everything. It looked like some kind of toxic nuclear waste site. The ground was like a swamp, sticky and soft like caramel. As Mark walked on the game room concrete, he saw that his avatar was having trouble. Mark had to take two or three steps to get Slowpry to take a single step forward.

There was a ceiling far above his head, but hills and ravines made of rocky materials were in the large area before him. There were no paths or routes that seemed to make sense, as though this were a huge warehouse of earth with a gunky, earthen floor. Decidedly unpleasant. Mark realized that his equipment included his rifle. He immediately reached back with his hand and found the plastic toy rifle in his backpack sleeve. He pulled the imitation weapon out, and the screen flashed the stage goal.

To survive, you must reach the power plant on the spaceship and turn it on. Your rifle has unlimited ammo, but do not jeopardize the integrity of the spaceship or you will all die.

It may only be a toy gun, but I might be able to overpower the guard.

Mark was much more concerned with his real life than with his avatar, although the end result would be the same—AK-47s or syringes.

Fellini sat at his circular desk, relishing the situation the impudent CIA agent now faced.

Mark was the first person to discover the truth about Ultimatus. But he will take that secret to his grave, Fellini mused contentedly.

Unbeknownst to Fellini, Gina also knew, making her the second person to know the truth. On Fellini's control-room screens, there were maps of the game but also screens with the GPS location of the Ultimus II. Corvo was on another screen; the ship was on course to return there at a very slow five knots. Fellini was always looking forward. He was a quick player in Ultimatus, as well as a chess master, always staying a step ahead of his opponents, even when it looked like his guard was down.

***

Simon watched the tournament as the final stage began. There was not much else to do in the office; a pall hung over everyone. When Fellini made his announcement, however, Simon leaped out of his chair, knocking it backward onto the ground. *Slowpry was alive!* This meant that they still had time to find Mark. He called Director Stewart as soon as he could think straight.

"Mrs. Ratner, I need to speak to him," Mark ordered her, more forceful than he'd ever been with the director's secretary.

"He's on a call."

"Interrupt him. Tell him that Mark is alive."

"What? He is?"

"Yes, now tell him!"

"Okay, hold on."

A few seconds later, Director Stewart cut in on the line.

"Simon, what is this about Mark being alive?"

"Sir, go to www.ultimatus.com. Slowpry was reinstated."

"You mean the avatar in the game?"

"Yes. Yes, sir."

"We can't be sure that this is, in fact, Mark. It could be someone else, right?" Robert asked.

"Technically? Yes, sir. But Mark could also be playing. We have no way of knowing what happened in the past eight hours. We have to resume the search," Simon pleaded.

"Okay, get them to run another pass over your best projected coordinates. A series of last sorties. Twenty-four hours max."

"Thank you, sir. Thank you."

Unfortunately, Simon's calculations of where the

Ultimus II was were all wrong. The ship was headed back to Corvo, a strategy that neither Simon nor Diaz had considered. The mission being locally led by Mr. Diaz had maps with bands of time fanned out from Corvo into huge swaths of the Atlantic Ocean, all in international waters. But the *Ultimus II* was already back in Portuguese waters, a few hours from the nearly deserted island of Corvo.

***

Slowpry was moving as slowly as his name suggested on his way up the nearest wall of debris and rock. A well-trained Navy Seal always moved to a location with as much visibility as possible.

At the top of the trash-compacted material mound, he surveyed the room of the ship. The long room had a hatch door on one end, another at the other end further away, and a series of windows on the opposite sides. The roof was strange, with a large rectangular skylight in the center pushed up higher than the actual ceiling. This was like the agricultural planting section of an abandoned spaceship gone horribly wrong.

Nice place to spawn! Marc thought sarcastically.

The plants were all dead, and the soil was probably toxic. Slowpry wondered how many players were in the space. He needed to determine the direction to the power plant. From the skylight, he might be able to see the whole ship, but the danger of being too exposed up there deterred him. He decided to move erratically, never stopping, in the direction of the nearest window. From a window, he might learn something more about his location on the ship. On his way up, he kept his gun out, with his finger on the trigger, in case another player lurked behind the next mound of earth or decrepit shrub formation. Paranoia set in, and his head was constantly on a distracting swivel. Slowpry eventually reached the large, round window without incident.

Empty space in every direction. No clues.

The noise from a snapped twig or piece of garbage reached his ear. He turned around to see a player pointing a rifle at him menacingly. Slowpry had the window behind him and pointed with his fingers at the glass as if saying, "don't shoot or we both die." The player was Noah88. Mark wondered what had made Noah88 hesitate. Fear? Maybe curiosity, as Slowpry had come back from digital death. He tried to speak, but Slowpry was unable; his communication system had been cut off by Fellini. Slowpry made signals pointing to his ears. Noah88 made other signals threatening to shoot if Slowpry didn't drop his weapon.

In the slight glare of his monitor, Mark saw the guard looking at his screen, intrigued by the predicament. The guard was unaware that Mark was watching him in the reflection. Mark planned to satisfy Noah88 in the game, but also needed to survive the guard and the inevitable needles. Slowpry moved slowly, showing Noah88 that he was not going to retaliate. He moved to drop the gun, but with a fast, jerking motion, he quickly chucked the weapon far to his right. Noah was confused, as this action posed no threat to him. In real life, Mark had launched the toy gun with all his might at the guard's forehead, stunning him and knocking him down. He immediately removed the Ultisuit backpack. The strange behavior and bizarre motions being made by Slowpry caused Noah88 to respond by shooting Slowpry dead on the spot. The count moved up to one.

Fellini watched the action in detail. He was sure that the Ultisuit would work this time, but the final movements of the avatar looked as though Slowpry was removing something from his back. One thing was certain, if Mark managed to pull away from the syringes, he still wouldn't be able to avoid the bullets from the guard's readied weapon. Fellini was not worried.

Mark successfully avoided the needles as they deployed, but wasn't fast enough to get to the guard before he cleared the stars from his eyes and raised his weapon. Mark didn't have the time or energy to engage a trained killer with an AK-47, so he opted to run out and leap over the window ledge to the concrete balcony and drop into the Atlantic Ocean before a bullet could catch him.

The yacht was moving slowly; he guessed around five knots, so he needed to quickly return and hook back to the structure before he was left stranded in the mid-Atlantic. Mark managed to slap a hand on one of the trailing pieces of the mock shantytown. He maneuvered back up onto the concrete pier with his left hand and immediately felt the strong pressure of the water like a water-skier before rising. He managed to pull himself back onto a horizontal support beam.

The guard was looking out from the edge of the boat, shouting and shooting at him, but the concrete wall and interlaced beam structure were ample protection. His next movement toward the main ship made the guard lose the angle, and he disappeared from view. Mark's only way back on the ship would be to return to the upper level where he had originally come from. He returned to the outside of the structure, where the guard had been shooting before, and, as expected, he found it empty.

Well, Fellini certainly knows now.

***

BlingBlingBaby was in a dark, dingy corridor of the spaceship. She was running away from a fallen player whom she had injured and knocked out cold. GustaffsonS was lying on the ground, waiting for the merciful end that never came. Gina was not about to kill any players now that she knew the true finality of the act.

She removed GustaffsonS's gun to avoid being shot in the back. The power-source goal was close; she had been lucky to spawn near its location. The reactor room was directly in front of her, hinted at by the ever-increasing number of cables aligned down the walls and ceiling of the hallway. She reached a closed hatch door that was shut with a keypad entry system. It was a glass area about the size of a sheet of paper. She placed her hand on the device, but nothing happened. She punched numbers, letters . . . nothing. Finally, she raised her rifle and released three rounds into the keypad. The door swung open, revealing the power room.

BlingBlingBaby found the main power source, which was a huge nuclear reactor with no apparent way to turn on. She walked all over the room but found no switches, levers, or control panels. Evidently, the way to start this beast was from the bridge, not here in the ship's bowels. Gina reevaluated her initial "lucky break." As always, these tournaments could be more challenging than they first appeared. She heard a lone shot from the hallway. Wounded by her, GustaffsonS was executed mercilessly by another player. The kill count moved to two. Gina's heart sank a bit further.

***

"What?" Fellini screamed at the guard.
"He is in the bowels of the structure."
"How could you leave him alive!"

"I, I . . . ."

"Just shut up."

Fellini ran toward his staircase to the bridge.

"Lock all the entries to the ship. Do it now!"

"Yes, sir."

"Captain Moraga. Full speed ahead—now."

I just can't kill this asshole. God, I hate him.

***

SodaPop was lying on the floor with his rifle aimed at the door of the control room when he felt the jolt of the ship changing speed. The floor shifted beneath him. He was prepared to shoot a player that was about to enter the control room, but both were jolted by the ship, and he lost focus for a moment. His opponent stumbled into his kill-box, and SodaPop took the shot, killing MessiMessi with a single round to the forehead. The death count moved up to three.

The control room was straight out of an alien movie. SodaPop couldn't figure out the computers in the bridge like some tech geek; it was definitely not his style. He had gotten this far because Ultimatus was not a game of geeky computers but a test of strategy and endurance. The bridge had to hold a clue to the power source, but if the computer screens were concealing this clue, SodaPop was the wrong player to find it. He surveyed the surroundings, keeping one eye always on the door in case another opponent arrived.

Eventually, he made up his mind. Deviously, he stood by the side of the door and waited for the next player to pop inside. He would capture them and use them to find what he had missed.

Always let others do the work for you, Ricardo reminded himself with a smile.

He used this popular saying all the time in his hometown of Mexico City. How far he was from his home and what danger he was in, yet he was completely oblivious to the true perils of the game. The noise from the creaking structure had become unbearable. The boat was moving much faster than in the second stage!

What the hell?

***

Mark knew that Fellini was after him. The speed the ship reached was twenty-six knots—quite fast. From the movement and sound coming from the structure, he wouldn't be surprised if the whole damn thing collapsed. Everyone was in danger as long as he remained on board.

Gina.

How the hell can I get off this ship?

Mark dangled from oxidized rebar on the bottom of the balcony floor of the furthest rear room of the structure. He grabbed the wall responsible for holding the structure together and carefully maneuvered to the other side. The rear of the yacht came into his view. The rear deck used for fishing and swimming gave him the opportunity he needed. Mark swung on the exposed rebar mistakes of the structure and hugged the wall by grabbing the holes left by the wood used during the pour. A large wooden stake that was still in place, never having been removed by the hurried builders, became his support to get onto the deck. The opportunity to jump to the safety of the ship also presented itself. He pushed himself off the wall and ceiling, grabbing the wooden stake but tearing the wood with his weight. By sheer luck, at that moment, he fell with both feet onto the handrail of the deck. In limbo for a second or two, he waited for the ship to rock in his favor before maneuvering forward to the deck.

Mark reached the large rear deck that connected to the boat via two sets of sliding doors. One was locked, but the other was open.

Sliding doors were always left open. Mark remembered this from his dad, who always complained about the doors in their house during the summer. *And pocket doors are never used . . . .*

He found the toy room on the same level, knowing that any attempt to move up into the main areas of the ship would likely get him killed. He was intrigued by the extensive depository of gadgets in this starboard storage area. He entered the room and closed the door behind him, securing the space by jamming the handle with a pole from a hang glider. In the room, a large submarine, three WaveRunners, a few kayaks, skis, and other toys lay unused, waiting to entertain. He found the large door that opened to the ocean, but was unsure if it would open with the ship moving at full speed. He still gave it a try. The large metal door slid open, although water quickly splashed up into the ship. The concrete structure in front of the toy room's sliding door had an opening clearly carved out to allow access to the open ocean.

Fellini wanted his submarine to be capable of launching, even with the main structure attached, Mark thought.

He tried to figure out the submarine, but realized that it required more than one person for the job. The submarine needed an operator to control the boom, which lowered the machine into the water.

A few decks above Mark's head, Fellini identified Mark's location, because the open side door flashed red on the captain's main screen. Fellini ordered the ship to slow down; the change in speed was gratefully noticed by all the players. Less than a minute later, Mark heard banging on the door; the guards were trying to break it down. The submarine idea was out, but he went for the next best thing, mounted a WaveRunner, and pushed it into the Atlantic. The concrete structure continued moving forward and pushed Mark off the vehicle into the cold water. Fortunately, the key remained attached, and when he clambered back on board, he got the WaveRunner revving and racing away in seconds.

Mark took off as fast as he could, heading directly away from the *Ultimus II*. The intense barrage against the door finally broke the aluminum pole and swung it open, revealing half a dozen guards and Fellini himself. They quickly moved to the door, looking for their quarry in the ocean. A guard spotted Mark's figure racing away and aimed his rifle. Fellini put his hand on the guard's barrel and lowered the gun.

"Don't waste your bullets. You're watching a dead man."

Mark was traveling on a WaveRunner with enough gas for fifty or sixty clicks, but his location was two-thousand clicks from anything. The *Ultimus II* slowed down to its five-knot speed toward Corvo. Mark was far from the ship before he stopped and realized that the shanty town was moving away from him at a much slower speed. He was slightly consoled by the idea that the structure wouldn't fall into the ocean, killing Gina and the remaining players. He stopped the engine of his recently stolen WaveRunner. Night was falling, and wasting gas would be a mistake. He stretched out on top of the

WaveRunner as best he could and tried to rest. His options? Limited.

Don't panic. Don't panic. Don't panic.

***

BlingBlingBaby was on a mission to find the main bridge of the spaceship. She peered into the open door and felt the cold circle of a barrel on her temple. Her wrist monitor pumped the signal, and on-screen she could see SodaPop's gun pressed against her head.

"Don't move," SodaPop said.

"I won't," BlingBlingBaby said, dropping her weapon immediately.

"I know what you're capable of, so don't try anything, or I'll end you," SodaPop threatened her.

"Ricardo, listen to me. We're all in grave danger. I know this sounds crazy, but the Ultisuit will kill you if you're killed in the game. We should not harm each other."

"Yeah, sure, BlingBling. Just help me start the power station so we can finish this thing."

"I just came from the power core. There were no levers . . . nothing. One of these computers must control this ship."

"Great. You find it and I'll guard the door," Ricardo replied, still wary of collaborating with BlingBlingBaby.

"Deal."

Gina was lucky that Fellini had not heard this exchange. He was too busy making sure that his CIA problem went away for good. As Fellini took a final look at Mark being left in the middle of the Atlantic on a WaveRunner, Gina continued her search.

This must be it, Gina decided as she located a hidden computer terminal that swung open like a laptop. She began to tap on various keys, but she couldn't start the device.

"I found the computer, but I can't make it work!" Gina said, half to herself and half to SodaPop.

"Damn. Well, in that case, I vote that we batten down the hatches and wait," Ricardo suggested.

"Fine. Just keep the door closed. Let me try to figure this out."

SodaPop closed the door and braced the handle with BlingBlingBaby's gun. He was nervous, but not nearly as much as she was. Gina was thinking about how to prevent more deaths. *But how?* She was all alone, and Mark had told her not to reveal anything to anyone.

However, a gun pressed to your head makes you break promises. She took a chance by telling Ricardo, and although he didn't seem to believe her, she didn't want to say anything more while in the game. The metal on her back gave her some security, but it was a false sense of security, as she had no idea what to do if the tray did save her.

Mark must be dead. The thought struck her like a physical blow.

The speed of the *Ultimus II* had returned to a serene flow, and that was the only explanation for things returning to "normal," She would have time to mourn in the future, but she needed to stay calm and pray that she wasn't perceived as a threat to Fellini's operation. She had the common sense not to try and rock the boat . . . yacht . . . spaceship. Whatever.

A shoulder collided with the door, and the handle

moved on the other side, clearly being forced by a desperate player. BlingBlingBaby ran to the door, and SodaPop stood on the other side. They both saw a clearly panicked Noah88. She signaled for him to drop his gun. Noah88, desperate and in need of help, dropped it without a second thought. BlingBlingBaby and SodaPop agreed to let him in; they both liked Noah88. The hatch door opened and Noah88 dove inside. They closed the hatch immediately; shots sparked off the metal as they slammed it shut.

"Whew . . . that was close. Thanks, guys," Noah said, pleased that they hadn't just shot him as soon as he stepped inside.

"No problem. If we survive, remind me to talk to you about something important," BlingBlingBaby said.

"Okay."

The count moved up to four. BlingBlingBaby called Noah88 over to the computer.

"I think this is the computer we need to turn the power source on, but I can't make it work," she said.

"Let me give it a shot."

***

Simon was determined to maintain the energy behind the search for the ship. The sorties from the *USS Eisenhower*, two-hundred clicks north of Corvo, had found nothing, and another day came to a close. Searching the open ocean at night was a waste of time, not to mention of gas and human resources. Daylight searching was the only possible way. Mr. Pedro Diaz called Simon from the *USS Eisenhower's* bridge.

"Simon? I'm afraid that the search is over. We couldn't find anything," Pedro told him somberly.

"Ships don't just disappear, Mr. Diaz."

"Well, this one has."

"Give the search one more day. The tournament isn't even over yet."

"We stopped searching when night fell. I will need clearance to start again tomorrow."

"You'll have it," Simon assured him.

"Alright, but make sure that I get the orders in writing before tomorrow, or General Marshall will not allow the planes to take off."

"You'll have it."

Simon called Director Stewart, but he was unavailable. He took matters into his own hands and headed straight for the director's office. Meanwhile, the sun set over the Atlantic Ocean, and Mark became sleepy. He closed his eyes after staring at the uninterrupted line of the horizon.

Mrs. Ratner kept working at her desk as Simon entered and greeted her in a lively manner. A second later, he turned visibly serious.

"What's happening, Simon?" she asked.

"You know that Mark is in danger, right?"

"He's a field operative, Simon."

"Yes, but this time, things are different. His cover is blown and he's on an enemy ship. He needs us."

"Well, what can I do for you?"

"I need Director Stewart to sign this order so that the search team can keep working tomorrow."

"But he left . . . ."

"I need this signed. Mrs. Ratner . . . please get this order to him. You're quite literally my only hope," Simon begged her.

"Okay . . . I'll do it."

Mrs. Ratner had the ability to reach Director Stewart

anywhere and at any time. Simon had counted on that. She sent the director a message via her computer with Simon standing before her. She received a quick reply text from Director Stewart. Mrs. Ratner winked at him and entered the director's office, closing the door behind her.

"Wait here."

On Director Stewart's desk, a small device with a fingerprint scanner on top sat largely unused. She placed the document in a slot on the device and on the glass screen, the placement of the signature on the paper below appeared. She aligned a red electronic box to the line with "Director Robert Stewart, CIA" written below it. Then she put her index finger on the glass, and the signature device scanned her identity, verified the fingerprint, and sent a tiny ballpoint pen on a path that signed the document exactly as if Director Stewart had done it himself. She exited his office and handed Simon the paper.

"Here you are," she said, clearly self-satisfied.

Simon looked down at the ink signature, which still looked wet.

"So he's here?"
"Yes, yes . . . " she told him unconvincingly.

Simon ran out to send the order to keep the search going the next morning.

***

Noah88 was searching for some clue of how to work this special computer amidst the chaos and filth of the control room. Noah had some knowledge of electrical gadgets from his father, and upon glancing at a circular protrusion near the desk, he had a revelation.

Bingo. It's like the Russian self-powered crank flashlight that my dad gave me.

Noah remembered the battery-free flashlight he received from his father back in San Diego. He fumbled with the device until he found a tiny arm that moved up from the center of the round circle and extended to the edge. After a few turns, this mini-generator powered the computer to life, and the power source activation button flashed on and off. The computer needed more power, so Noah88 cranked harder.

The count moved up to five.

Somewhere in the structure, a newbie called KhoshTip had been killed. Fellini would soon enter KhoshTip's game cubicle to send him to the bottom of the Atlantic tied to a slab of concrete. His feet would be secured by the plastic ties, and his lungs would quickly fill with water, the paralysis forbidding any possibility of survival.

Gina knew that this happened but still found it hard to imagine Ultimatus living up to the rumors. She even considered letting herself be killed to see the deployed syringes. She had been struck by KhoshTip at their last meal—by his exotic, quiet beauty, which his avatar name implied in Farsi.

Maybe I can take an Ultisuit with me when I leave. Proof!

BlingBlingBaby, Noah88, and SodaPop were released from the game by clicking the computer power-source button. Each one was sent to their individual victory ceremonies. They were officially champions! Noah88 and SodaPop were both thrilled that they'd reached the end of the journey, but their excitement was tempered by the aura that something still wasn't right.

They were not summoned to leave the game room; they needed to stay for the kill count to reach six and experience the final ceremony. However, they were safe. Waiting for another young player to be killed made Gina furious and depressed. She didn't want to know who would die next.

The door to the control room was banged on again, but with no one inside to open it and BlingBlingBaby's gun still jamming the handle, the situation was dire. Pounding her fist on the hatch was a newbie by the name of OliviaNJ. She knocked desperately until a single shot found her skull.

The count ended; six dead in the game. Five were dead at the bottom of the Atlantic Ocean, while the sixth death was still paradoxically alive, floating on a WaveRunner in the middle of the ocean without any possibility of reaching land—no food, no water . . . dead.

All computer monitors flashed, and the final game-over ceremony commenced with the scrolling names of the eliminated players:

Slowpry - Spielberg
GustaffsonS - Wilder
MessiMessi - Martel
GuptaGita - Egoyan
KhoshTip - Kiarostami
OliviaNJ - Miller

Immediately after the scrolled names, the screen showed the spaceship in which they had been battling in outer space. Then, the camera panned, revealing Earth beyond. The image zoomed in all the way to the East Coast of the United States, down to New York City's East

River, continuing even further down to the terrace of the United Nations Building complex.

All the presidents and ambassadors of the world, in digital animation, were standing on the plaza with flags from every nation flapping on their flagpoles. The ten avatars of the winners stood on a raised platform, being cheered by the dignitaries. A list scrolled the names of the avatars and with their new or remaining level names. Noah88, SodaPop, and SintraChamp were all moving up to level nine although to them it was the highest director level possible in their sphere.

Noah88 - Kubrick
BlingBlingBaby - Visconti
SodaPop - Iñarritu
Nachomaster - Egoyan
Chirripo29 - Gomez
SintraChamp - De Oliveira
Maheraha - Truffaut
KatoLee - Kurosawa
Loyang1 - Khoo
DunedinAA - Campion

The ceremony included fireworks and images of victory from various movies and news reels throughout history. The avatars looked happy and were smiling broadly, something they couldn't do in normal gameplay. The players back at the ship were being escorted out of the game rooms; the staff was already removing the Ultisuits and monitors from the game room walls as they moved back to the yacht. The tournament gaming paraphernalia all had to be moved back on board the *Ultimus II*. Fellini's image appeared on the screen in the living room; he delivered the usual congratulatory speech. Most people watching the show were now waiting for the traditional highlight reel of the best moments, so he knew that he had a captive audience.

"Players and citizens of the world, the 5th Ultimatus Tournament has been a success. Never before have so many new players reached the highest level. Three Ultimatus champions have lost their position. Firemist1 will be sorely missed after his last four tournament appearances, as well as StealthUfo, a three-time champ, and ProntoCall. The new winners, however, will enjoy a brand-new level of fame and will continue to spread the word about Ultimatus to future champions. Congratulations to all of you players, and a special congratulations to Noah88, SodaPop, and SintraChamp. Now, what you've all been waiting for . . . here are the most exciting highlights of the 5th Annual Ultimatus Tournament!"

Reruns of the best moments and the best kills or defensive maneuvers flowed across the screen. Many different camera angles depicted the moments in dramatic fashion, and the action was enhanced by slow-motion kill shots and fantastic high-definition imagery.

Gina couldn't watch the images of the violence being celebrated by millions around the world who had no idea they were essentially watching real people being killed. The gruesome detail of the videos sent a wave of nausea through her body. She headed to her room before the reruns ended. All of the other players were glued to the screen, watching the highlights intently in the yacht's plush living room.

Gina also needed to avoid someone detecting her use of the metal tray. Once in her room, she took the safety device off and hid the serving tray under the bathroom sink cabinet. She jumped in the shower to clean off the layers of grime and sweat that had been built up on her skin—this stage had obviously been more intense than the others. In fact, this had been the scariest day in her whole life.

Fellini was truly a monster. She thought about not leaving her room for dinner and skipping the party. How could she act normal and interact with the nine other winners when she knew the real fate of the other twenty? At the same time, she knew that she needed to pretend that all was well—her life depended on it.

I'll warn more players once we get off this damn boat.

16

Fellini gave the captain the order to stop about an hour after the tournament finished. The ten winners were beginning to gather in the dining room and noted the speed change. The captain pressed a switch that detonated the C-4 charges. The center of each beam that held the shantytown over the yacht exploded. The force broke the four main beams, and the structure was shed instantly. The beams shot up like wooden matchsticks being split between fingers and rolled onto eight side-rollers specifically made for this purpose. The structure had been designed to fall into the ocean, away from the ship and its parapet walls. The entire structure fell into the Atlantic, never to be seen again. The two large inflatable canvas bags floated on top of the ocean; they had helped support the weight of the structure and prevented falling debris from hitting the hull of the ship. The captain of the ship briskly exited the bridge and punctured both bags with two well-placed shotgun blasts. Slowly, they released their air and would also eventually sink.

Another piece of Atlantis, Fellini thought, pleased that his meticulous planning was still working.

The players were slightly awed by the rapid transformation of the yacht and were happy to see the stars and the ocean again. The ship seemed to return to the luxurious pleasure cruise that they had enjoyed at the beginning of their adventure. They drank and celebrated freely, never mentioning the missing players. Gina knew that she could be under the watchful eye of Fellini, so she tried to play her part and look cheerful about being a four-time champion. Finally, the party wound down. The players eventually peeled off to sleep in their cabins on the *Ultimus II,* which was traveling east at twenty-five knots. Without the additional structure to haul, the ship felt light, and it cut through the waves like a knife. Their destination wouldn't take long to reach at that speed: Corvo, Azores Archipelago, Portugal.

***

Stranded in the Atlantic Ocean, about one-hundred-and-eighty kilometers from the nearest island, Mark was cooking in the heat of the sun. He was on the WaveRunner, listening intently to the earth, trying to detect the noise of any vessel—a plane, a boat . . . he didn't care. He was sitting on the handlebars; in front of him was the disabled machine he had taken apart. He had removed the seat and taken the battery out from the bowels of the machine. He hooked wires to the positive and negative charges and prepared to connect those wires. He removed all of the black, rubber bumper from around the machine and placed it in the engine cavity, careful not

217

to get it too wet.

He looked at his watch; it was nearly 8 a.m. He had waited through a long night for this chance, and by all his estimates, 8 a.m. seemed like the time that a rescue airplane might be nearby. He took off his T-shirt, opened the gas tank, and inserted the fabric. He pulled the shirt out, damp with gas, and wet the underbelly of the seat that he had flipped and placed in a perpendicular position to the boat. He carefully touched the two cables together, sending sparks falling onto the oil-soaked rag.

The shirt and the plastic foam of the seat caught fire quickly. Mark played it cool, not wanting to get overexcited and make a mistake. He grabbed a long rubber bumper and ignited the tip of the black flammable plastic with the fire created by the gasoline. The rubber burned hot and dripped the molten plastic of its petroleum-based composition. The effect caused a plume of toxic black smoke to rise from the WaveRunner high into the sky. It was a disgusting, acrid plastic flame that Mark needed to control and maintain for as long as he could. His only hope for survival was that someone, somewhere, would see the signal.

He burned all the rubber from the bumpers, the seat, the plastic handlebars, and the rubber parts in the engine—everything he could possibly burn until there was almost nothing left.

***

About fifteen kilometers off the coast of Corvo, a large, beautiful yacht stopped. Inside its luxurious quarters, ten Ultimatus champions were sleeping. Fellini, however, had always been an early riser.

He was in the toy storage of the yacht, already

strapped inside the miniature submarine. The submersible was being maneuvered into the sea by an assistant manipulating the huge metallic arm. When it disengaged, the submarine sank gently, giving Fellini a perfect underwater view in dry and surprisingly comfortable conditions. He had also added two large mechanic arms in front of the vehicle, which he tested as he moved the steel tube forward through the water.

***

Mark had burned everything he could possibly burn. The last flammable item was the WaveRunner itself. He jumped into the water and quickly shoved the positive cable into the gas tank, followed by the negative one, before diving beneath the waves. The tank, full of fumes, exploded within seconds. After hearing the blast, Mark emerged from the water as the last smoke he would be able to create rose up in the air. That last effort hadn't been ideal, because the WaveRunner quickly sank. The explosion must have opened up a hole on the undercarriage. Mark swam to the floating seat and used it to remain afloat and wait for the help that might never come.

A few minutes earlier, a US F-16 pilot had flown his last search mission for the *Ultimus II*. He flew the route at about one thousand feet and was turning toward the *USS Eisenhower* when the pilot saw a puff of black smoke in the air. He circled lower and approached the point when his radar detected a small explosion on the water. He passed at high speed, at an altitude of just over one hundred feet and spotted Mark floating in the endless blue. He quickly called in the coordinates.

Now they just need to reach me before the sharks do . . . .

***

A certain beach in Italy, called Forte dei Marmi, was the summer spot for most Florentines wanting to get out of the city. On that stunning sandy beach, people swam in the spectacular sea, lounged in the sun, and enjoyed their summers eating baked pizzas and drinking cold Peronis. Life in August was sweet at Forte dei Marmi. In the water, the most remarkable thing to admire was the array of beautiful women, but at the end of the Ultimatus Tournament, beach-goers were instead staring at a strange yellow blob that had appeared under the sea.

The yellow mass rose slowly and steadily as it came closer to the sandy beach. From the top of the blob, a round portion rose above the sea level by about a foot. A hatch opened and from inside, a gorgeous woman in a bikini ascended, as if from an elevator, and jumped into the water. Behind her, a young man did the same, and then another, and another. They swam to the beach and walked past gaping tourists to reach the main street, crossing the avenue to the side streets full of homes and small hotels. Gina walked barefoot and wet into the small lobby of the Hotel Pigionet and strode directly to the front desk.

"Gina Gazzoni."

"One moment," the hotel employee replied, his mouth hanging slightly agape.

"What's the room number?" Gina asked hurriedly.

The man stared at her blankly, as though he hadn't heard the question.

"Room. Number." Gina was annoyed.

"Oh, of course . . . 134" he replied, shamefacedly.

She took her room card and walked away, the gaze of the idiotic front-desk clerk locked on her bouncing behind. The men followed one at a time into the Pigionet, where each demanded their room. One woman and nine men made a total of ten new guests.

In her room, Gina found her passport, clothes, and other possessions organized in the bathroom. She showered and sank into the bed. Her senses still perceived the bed to be moving with the rhythm of the Atlantic Ocean, but that sensation eventually faded. She knew that this year, her transition back to real life would not be like other post-tournament periods.

She slept, completely exhausted. Her dreams were disturbed by all the death surrounding her gaming life. She also woke up with an awful thought that wouldn't leave her for many years.

Why didn't I throw the tray out the window?

Later that night, she went downstairs and found Noah and Ricardo chatting in the hotel restaurant. She joined them.

"Did he tell you, Noah?" Gina asked, looking back and forth between the two.

"What?" Noah asked.

"I didn't tell him, Gina. I still don't know what to think. I mean, I believe you, but I didn't want to start spreading rumors to everyone," Ricardo said sheepishly.

Gina gave Ricardo a stern look and then turned to Noah, who clearly had no idea what they were talking about. "Listen, Noah. The game was real when we played on the ship."

"I know. It was intense," he replied slowly.

"No, listen. The people that we killed playing the game were actually murdered. By the Ultisuit."

"Wait . . . what? What are you talking about? Are you trying to tell me that the Ultimatus rumors are true?"

"That's my point. We sort of . . . just thought they were rumors. The language in the contract has always been vague, describing full consequences but never death. Fellini had the eliminated players injected with poison, tied to concrete blocks, and dropped to the bottom of the ocean. I'm never going back to the tournament again."

"Even if that's true . . . what about the money? I worked hard to get here," Noah argued with that fierce stubbornness that only a twenty-something who had just been given a golden ticket could muster.

"All I can tell you is that you're in much greater danger than you think. Play for a year, but when your ticket comes for the next tournament . . . don't go. Keep the money. Save it. Invest it. Whatever."

"One million euros is enough for me. In Mexico, a million euros is like winning the lottery," Ricardo explained.

"Just to let you know, I'm not going to play anymore. I did love meeting you guys though. Be careful," Gina warned them, but then dropped her head into her hands in a very un-BlingBlingBaby-like move.

"Likewise, but why are you crying! What is it?" Ricardo tried to comfort her.

"I just lost a lot of people I cared about in the past few days—and in the past few years. Some of them I even loved."

"Mark?" Noah guessed.

Gina looked at him in surprise for a moment and then nodded.

"Stellan, too!" she sobbed as his name came out of her mouth.

"I can't believe they're really dead," Noah breathed in shock, still processing his own actions and what they meant.

Gina rose and left with another few words of farewell. She needed to find proof for the police to stop

Fellini. A vision of a soaking wet Stellan crumpled at the bottom of the ocean tied to a concrete block came into her mind. Although it horrified her, it also made her pause.

When the first ten players died, we were not on open sea. I know the location of those bodies. I need to contact the Florentine Interpol office.

17

Mark was on board the *USS Eisenhower*, freshly
rescued and warm. He was wearing a fresh sailor's
uniform when an F-16 landed on the deck. A fighter pilot
and Simon, dressed as shabbily as always, descended from
the cockpit. Mark and Simon looked at each other; Simon
was nearly in tears but was trying to hold them in.

"You absolute bastard. You had me worried,"
Simon said, working on being tough rather than
emotional.

"You were worried? Well boo-hoo! I thought you
left me for dead!" Mark said, teasing his reluctant partner.

"Yes, granted, you had the tougher job. But believe
me, sitting at a desk and watching you die on screen—
twice—was not exactly a walk in the park. We were all
glued to the screen."

"We?"

"Practically the whole bureau."

"Director Stewart?"

"During the whole tournament."

Mark and Simon kept talking as the ship approached their destination. This was not a reunion, but rather a search mission. They were on course for Corvo.

"You know, your sloppiness and lack of professionalism cost me another date with Patricia," Simon said jokingly.

"What? You're unbelievable. I almost died yet you still blame me for *your* lack of social skills. You're a real trip."

Mark punched Simon in the shoulder, like an older brother.

"Ouch, Jesus. I'm just kidding."
"So what happened with Patricia?"
"I stood her up. Again."
"If she loves you, then she'll look the other way."
"We'll see."

***

Onboard the *Ultimus II*, the staff and Fellini were safely moving east through the Bosporus Strait, on course for Odessa, where maintenance for the huge yacht had been scheduled. Fellini was editing the tournament and checking stats to launch a huge Facebook, Twitter, Google, Instagram, and YouTube campaign. Each year, the corporation spent more and more on publicity, and the venues grew ever more diverse and expensive. In Istanbul, he would pick up account executives from all of his vendors as well as his publicity and advertising guru from BBDO.

Ultimatus relied on this publicity to bring in hundreds of thousands of new accounts every year. Running a billion-euro corporation created the same responsibilities as any other large enterprise, and Fellini was not stopping, or even slowing, his quest for gaming supremacy.

An assistant entered Fellini's office, carrying the tray found in Gina's room.

"Sir, we found this tray in the bathroom of cabin 23," the assistant reported.
"Give it to me."

Once the woman had left the room, Fellini quickly inspected the tray and noticed the twelve scratch marks on the back. Only one thing could have made them.

She knows.

***

At the makeshift pier on the uninhabited side of Corvo, a team of divers surfaced and signaled that they had found nothing. Simon and Mark were standing by the pier, disappointed at the lack of evidence. It would take more than Mark and Gina's word to mobilize and motivate Interpol and police around the world. A body would help and would also give closure to the many families in the sad situation of having a missing child. Fellini knew that no case could be brought against the Ultimatus Corporation based on the word of a previous gamer. The mystery surrounding the vanished players also brought the game more publicity and more news coverage. Even if the news was bad or controversial, all news was good for profits.

Fellini had already returned to Corvo before the *USS Eisenhower*. He had used his mini-submarine and its robotic arms to drag the ten bodies, one at a time, to another distant area where they wouldn't be found. The ocean was so big that a mere hundred meters was enough to hide anything. The bodies were also biodegradable and fish in the area loved them, so within a week, possibly two, there wouldn't be anything left to prove that Ultimatus was fulfilling its contractual promise. No hard evidence meant no conviction. Fellini was not a fool.

Mark and Simon decided to find Gina Gazzoni. They knew that she could possibly be in danger due to her contact with Mark and her knowledge of the truth behind Ultimatus. The two men flew from Corvo to Florence thanks to Mrs. Ratner and her magic signature pad. They had no clue where they might find her, so they began by visiting the Interpol office to see if they had any idea of her whereabouts. The old government building was an architectural marvel and sported a massive wooden door that was always kept open. Mark walked in confidently, followed by Simon, who identified himself to the agent.

"I'd like to speak with the Head of International Crime – Cybercrime Division," Simon stated calmly.
"That would be Signore Pasolini. One moment, gentlemen," the receptionist said in an accent that reminded Mark of Gina if he closed his eyes.

At the same time, Gina Gazzoni was actually in the building, sitting in an office with Mr. Pasolini, his assistant, and a Swedish officer, Ingeborg Larsson. Detective Inspector Eric Bergstrom had sent her to investigate more on Ultimatus and Firemist1's death. Eric's in-depth monitoring of the game led him to believe that BlingBlingBaby knew Firemist1; also, Florence was the closest city to Sweden with a repeat champion. Gina was recounting the story of Mark, the CIA, the syringes, and the death traps on the yacht. They all stared at her in disbelief; admittedly, the story sounded like the best kind of fiction.

Mark and Simon waited outside the main office

entrance but were soon following a shapely Italian policewoman as she weaved through a large room of cubicles that was surrounded by glass-walled offices on the periphery. They walked down the main corridor when a scream pierced the low hum of the office from behind one of the glass walls. A few officers leaped to their feet, guns drawn. The door next to Mark and Simon was thrown open.

"Slowpry!" Gina called.
"Gina?" Mark asked, genuinely speechless.

Gina ran out of Inspector Pasolini's office and practically tackled Mark; for a moment, it looked as though she was going to attack him. Instead, they kissed passionately, as if they were alone in the heavily populated room. A massive weight lifted from her shoulders.

"I can't believe you're alive . . . how?" Gina said, shocked.

Simon and various Interpol officers shyly shared a moment of both jealousy and curiosity.

"Gina, meet Simon. He's the one responsible for almost getting me killed by Fellini!" Mark teased him. "I have so much to tell you!"
"Hi there," Simon said nervously.

Simon shook Gina's hand, but she leaned in, expecting to be kissed on both cheeks. It was awkward.

"Hello, Simon."
"How are you holding up?"
"I've been a wreck, but now I'm better, having Mark here. These inspectors here, Pasolini, my God! He doesn't believe a word of my story. Please, Simon . . . talk to him. They say that we have no evidence," Gina explained.

"I'll talk to Pasolini . . . but he may be right. We just got back from Corvo. We didn't find anything. Mark, tell her about Corvo," Simon said as he headed for the open doorway to Pasolini's office.

Mark explained the lack of physical evidence on the ocean floor. Gina was unsurprised, knowing that Fellini was always a step ahead in his personal chess game. Her face fell but for a different reason.

"Mark . . . I made a huge mistake," Gina confessed.
"What?"
"I left the tray in the bathroom cabinet of my cabin." Mark's face fell just as deeply as hers.
"Damn! Well, we need to get you out of your apartment—away from your old life," Mark immediately decided.
"But do you really think that Fellini would take that chance?" Gina asked, thinking of what giving up her old life would mean.
"I'm not going to take that chance."

Mark embraced her, and Gina felt safe for the first time in days.

Through the glass, she could see Pasolini nodding, occasionally looking through the window between her and Mark. His incredulous face was a delight to Gina, considering that he had not believed a single scrap of her story only a few minutes before. Then Gina's eyes met Ingeborg's, and she saw what grief looked like on the face of a pretty Swede. Ingeborg was listening to Simon as the CIA agent detailed the awful truth. Stellan had died in the game, but Ingeborg remembered who had killed him. It all sunk in, slamming home the reality of his death; she stormed out of the meeting, straight toward Gina and Mark.

"You're Slowpry?" Ingeborg asked.

"Yes."

"You bastard!" She launched herself at Mark, and he grabbed her hands to stop her from striking him. She was sobbing uncontrollably. Gina sensed that this was the woman responsible for Stellan's attitude with her that first night on the ship.

"I couldn't save him. I swear . . . I tried." Mark consoled her in the only way he knew how—with the truth.

Ingeborg's legs failed her, and she collapsed to the floor. Gina squatted, sat on the floor, and held her tightly.

"Ingeborg?" Gina asked.

"How do you know my name?"

"Because Stellan was an old friend of mine. I was one of the last people to see him alive. I want you to know that he loved you very much."

"What? How could you possibly know that?"

"Because he talked to me about you. He wanted to marry you. For what it's worth. He was a good man."

Ingeborg felt some measure of relief; that knowledge gave her some desperately needed strength. She stood up and apologized to Mark. She understood that the players in the game were not actually responsible for the death of other players. That responsibility was squarely on the cruel shoulders of Fellini.

18

Mark and Gina were inseparable after their chance meeting at the Florence Interpol office. From that point forward, their relationship was based on two strong foundations: their love for each other and their hatred for Fellini. Two bonds that intense were more than most people had. Fellini stopped paying Gina her monthly paycheck the moment he found the metal tray in her room.

When Gina sold the apartment in Florence and paid the bank note, Fellini confirmed that she was gone from Ultimatus forever. Gina tried to close the BlingBlingBaby account on the Ultimatus server, but she found it impossible. Fellini had altered the password, so BlingBlingBaby remained active. Fellini considered Gina an enemy now, so his best strategy was not to eliminate

her outside of the game, but inside it. By keeping
BlingBlingBaby active, the general public would see her go
on, and in the upcoming annual tournament he could have
her easily eliminated in the first round. Then she would be
dead to Ultimatus with the whole world watching.

Having a champion defect was unacceptable to both
Fellini and the game's reputation. Fellini was not about to
be deterred by the actions of a few rogue players.

**

Upon returning to Langley, Simon began daily
training to achieve the stamina and physique required to
play Ultimatus. The Langley gym, where agents kept fit,
was a good place for his training regimen, because the
levels of competition and instruction were some of the
best in the world. Simon was working on his new plan to
stop Fellini. He could no longer use BlingBlingBaby or
Slowpry, so he was preparing his next best option. He
called in his two new CIA recruits, Noah Jones and
Ricardo Rodriguez, otherwise known as Noah88 and
SodaPop, respectively. If his new avatar, HermesHap,
managed to earn an invitation, then Simon's team would
have three agents infiltrating the Ultimatus tournament the
following year.

**

At the same time, halfway around the world, Fellini
was already preparing for the next tournament. With a
single click, he made all Kubrick-, Spielberg-, Bergman-,
Arden-Oplev-, Visconti-, and Bertolucci-levels vulnerable
by removing their ability to enter the tournament. This
took care of any possible entry by agents of the American,
Swedish, or Italian governments. As different countries
got closer to uncovering Ultimatus's secrets, the necessary
steps needed to be taken.

***

Director Stewart never received a complete, comprehensive hierarchy of the game's director levels from Simon. Instead, the report explained how Fellini-level was the highest and how most champions were on one level below yet the highest possible for them, a few more players on the third, and so on. Simon's promise remained unfulfilled, because no computer at the CIA could find an algorithm that linked the various directors' last names and the avatar names of the players. It was impossible to decipher a connection without the main parameters that Fellini used, which were in his sole possession: IP addresses & his directors lists in order of best to worst for any given country. Players knew their particular order of ascension as they where told different goals by the game depending on their geographic location. The information of these whereabouts was impossible to cross-reference with avatar names as kids routinely named their avatars the weirdest possible names they could muster.

***

Fellini was already planning a new location for the 6th Annual Tournament. He needed one that would give him at least thirty hours of time before any governmental search operations could reach him.

Maybe an abandoned mine? Only one cable would need to come out and feed the satellite. Batteries could be used to power the whole tournament beneath the earth. Why not? I could leave the dead inside and only extract the winners. It would be a perfect tomb with a little C-4. Next time, the tournament will be impenetrable and I will monitor it remotely.

The chess game had only just begun.

THE END

ABOUT THE AUTHOR

A. A. Dober wrote *Ultimatus: A Gaming Corporation* in 2013. It is his debut novel.
He lives in California.

www.ingramcontent.com/pod-product-compliance
Lightning Source LLC
LaVergne TN
LVHW042138040326
832903LV00011B/293/J